Aylmer Ontario Book 2 in Colour Photos, Saving Our History One Photo at a Time

Photography
by Barbara Raué
2014

Series Name:
Cruising Ontario

Book 79: Aylmer Book 2

Cover photo: 24 Pine Street

Series Name: Cruising Ontario
Saving Our History One Photo at a Time

Other Books by Barbara Raue

Coins of Gold

Arrows, Indians and Love

The Life and Times of Barbara
Volume 1: Inventions That Have Enhanced My Life
Volume 2: Entertainment That I Have Enjoyed
Volume 3: East Coast Trips
Volume 4: Olympics Have Always Intrigued Me
Volume 5: Wonders of the World
Volume 6: Caribbean Cruises We Have Enjoyed
Volume 7: Animals
Volume 8: Storms and Other Major Disasters in My Lifetime
Volume 9: Wars, Terrorist Attacks and Major Disasters

The Cromwell Family Book

Laura Secord Discovered

Visit Barbara's website to view all of her books
http://barbararaue.ca

Aylmer

Aylmer is located in southern Ontario just north of Lake Erie on Catfish Creek. It is 20 kilometers south of Highway 401. It is located on Highway 3 between St. Thomas to the west, and Tillsonburg to the east.

In October 1817, John Van Patter, an emigrant from New York State, obtained 200 acres of land and was the first settler on the site of Aylmer. During the 1830s a general store was opened and village lots sold.

Originally called Troy, in 1835 it was renamed Aylmer after Lord Aylmer, then Governor-in-Chief of British North America. By 1851 local enterprises included sawmills and flour-mills powered by water from Catfish Creek.

By the mid-1860s Aylmer, with easy access to Lake Erie, became the marketing center for a rich agricultural and timber producing area. Aylmer benefited greatly from the construction of the 145-mile Canada Air Line Railway from Glencoe to Fort Erie.

The coming of the Great Western Air Line railway in 1873 encouraged manufacturing and mills, a foundry, a pork-packing house, a milk-evaporating plant, and shoe factory were among the main establishments. An Airfield for training was established nearby in World War 2 which became the nucleus of the Ontario Police College.

The Aylmer Canning Factory was established in 1879; it packed peas, beans, cider, pickles, vinegar, sauces, meats and fruits.

Imperial Tobacco Canada built a plant in 1945. At its peak, it employed more than 600 full-time and seasonal workers. In its prime, the plant could store 110 million tons of tobacco and had an October to April production capacity of 100 million tons. Of this, 20 to 25 million tons were for export to other countries, making it one of Canada's leading exporters. The rest of the processed tobacco was shipped to Imperial's cigarette production plant in Guelph. After declining tobacco sales in Canada, Imperial began downsizing in the 1990s and closed in 2007.

Table of Contents

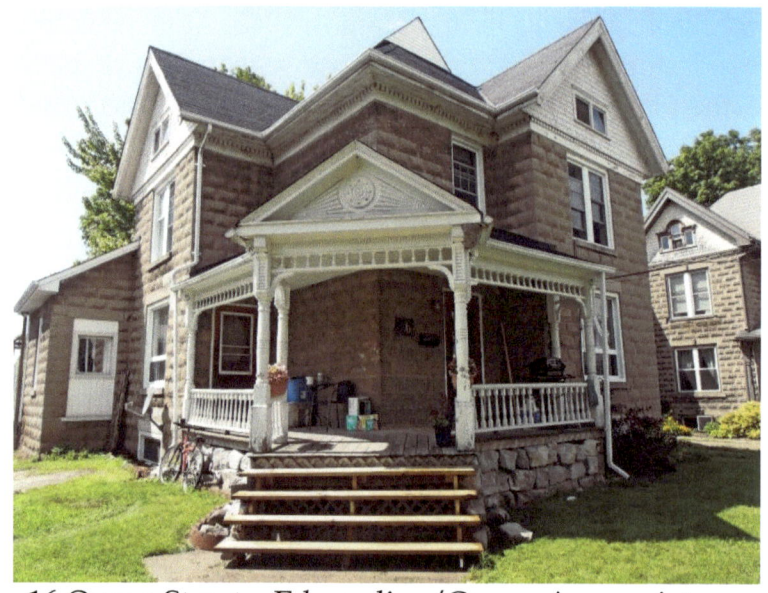

16 Queen Street – Edwardian/Queen Anne mixture, pediment

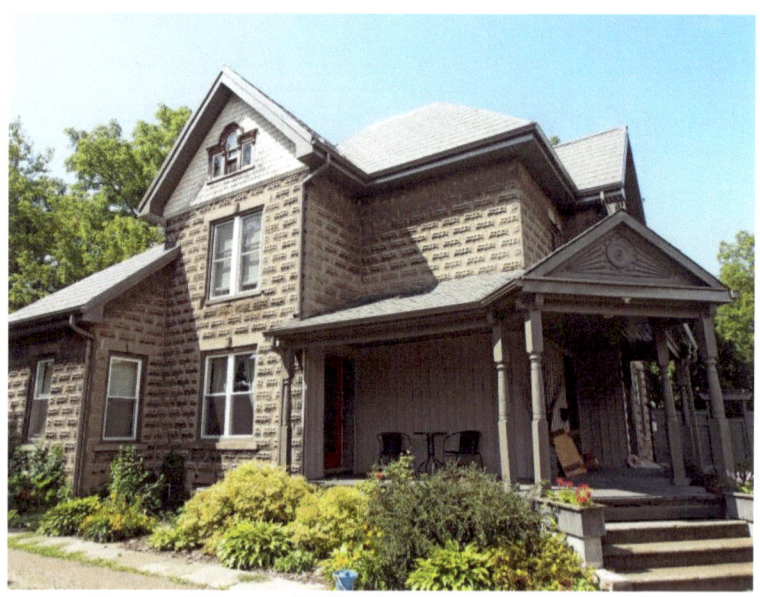

Queen Street – Palladian window in gable, pediment with decorated tympanum

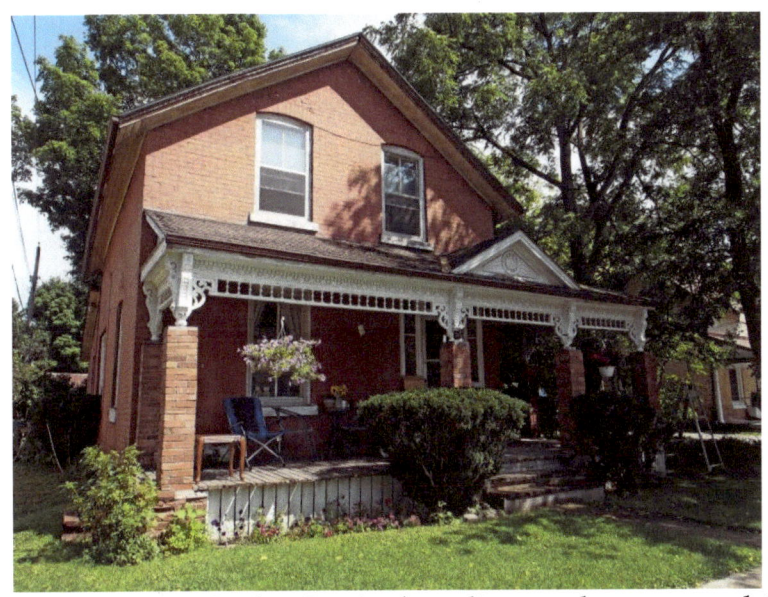

7 Elgin Street – Gothic Revival, pediment above verandah

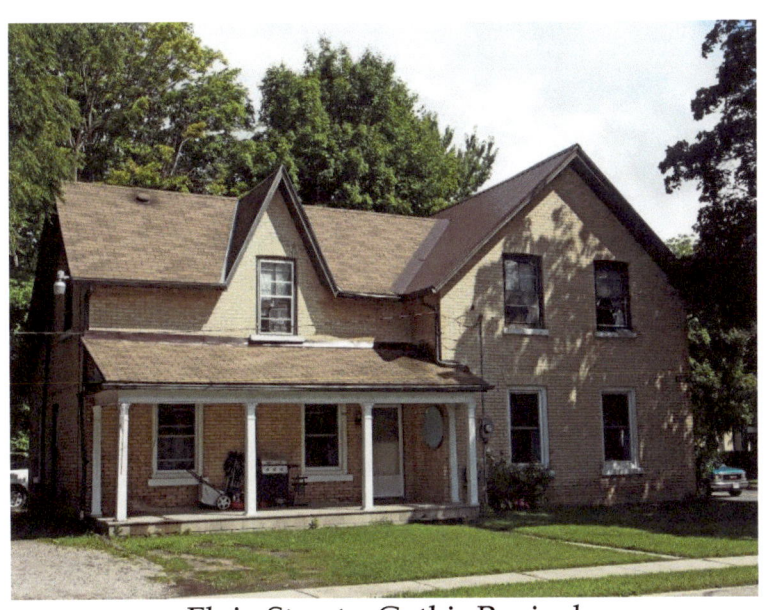

Elgin Street – Gothic Revival

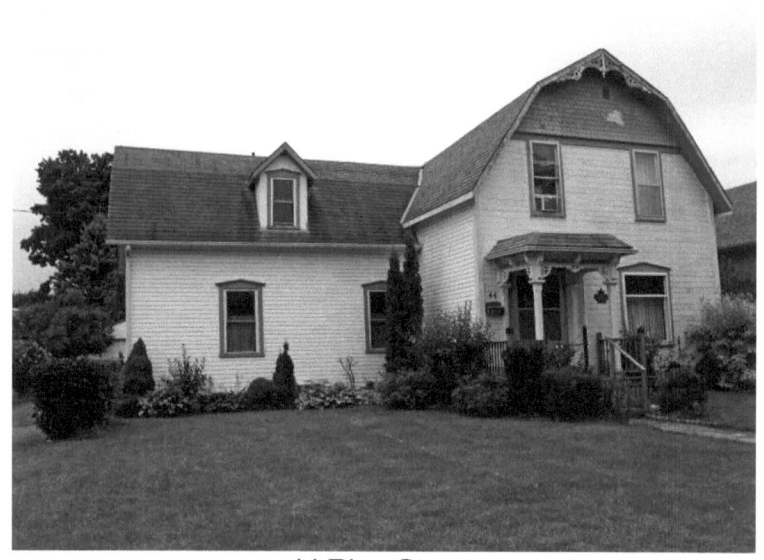

44 Pine Street

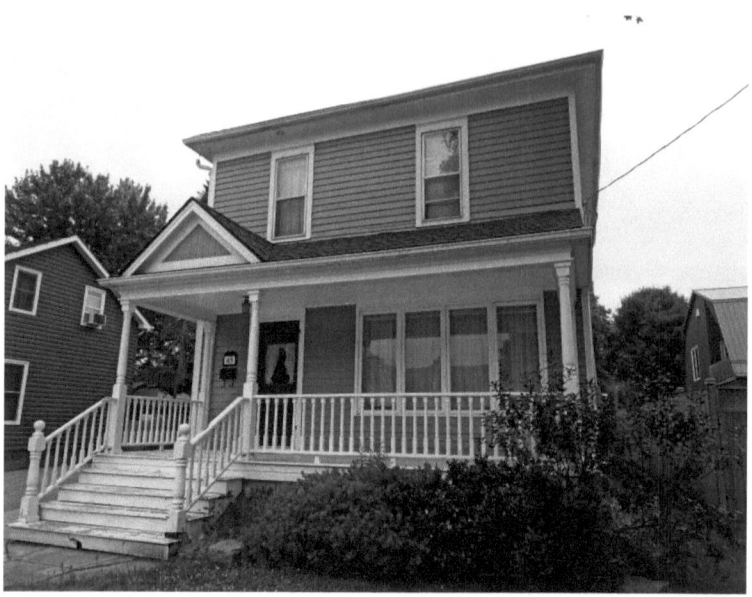

45 Pine Street – Italianate, pediment above verandah

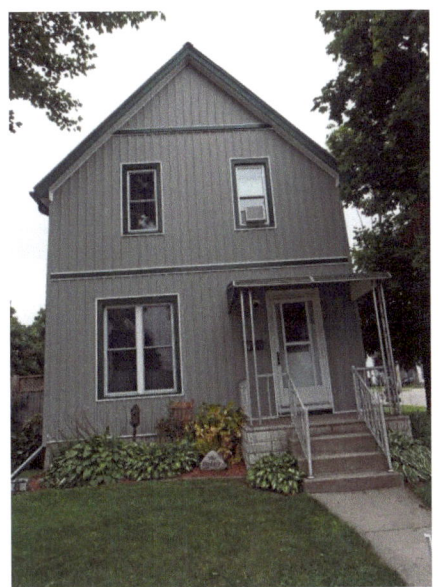

49 Pine Street – Gothic Revival

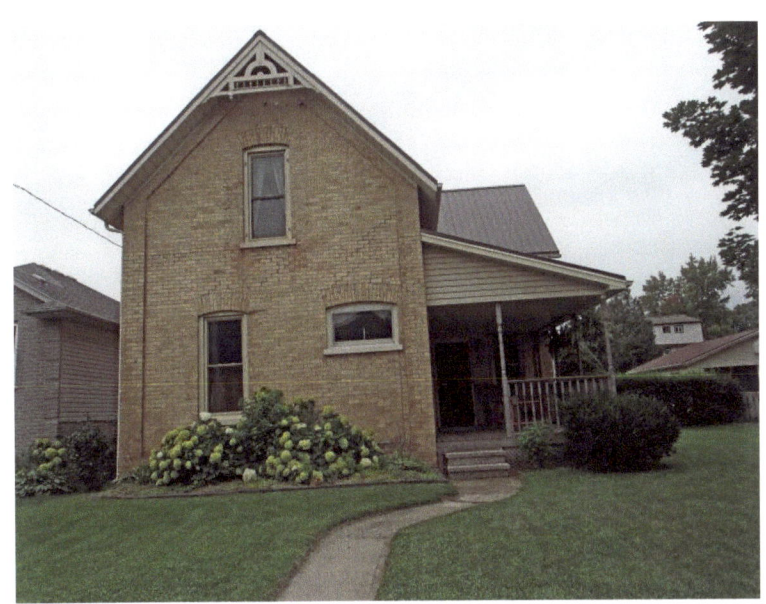

38 Pine Street - Gothic Revival, vergeboard trim on gable

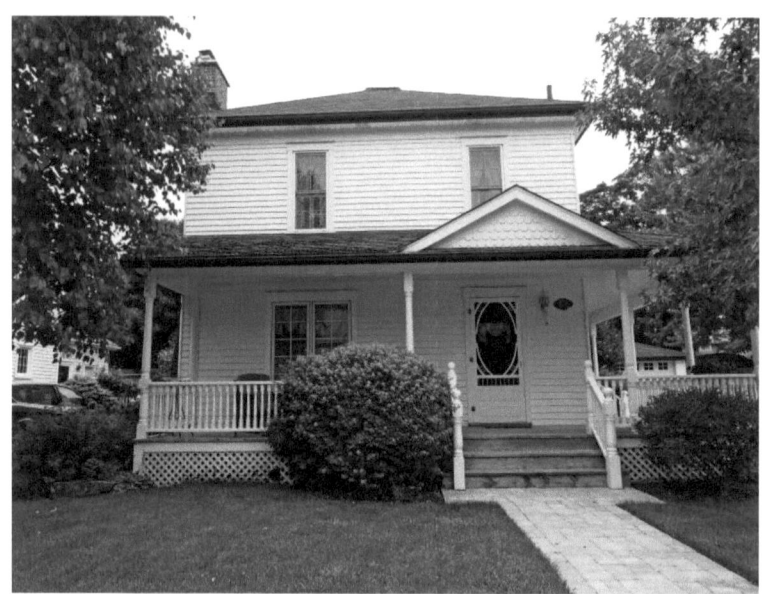

37 Pine Street – Italianate, hipped roof, pediment

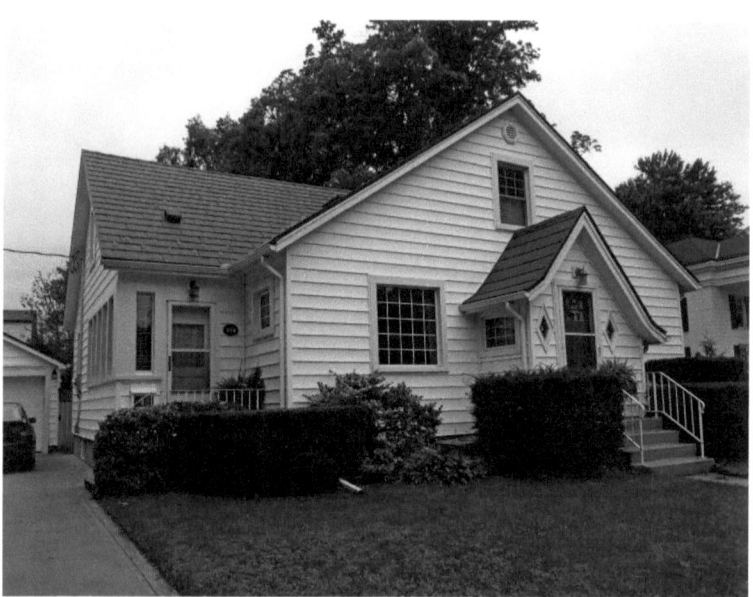

28 Pine Street – Gothic Revival

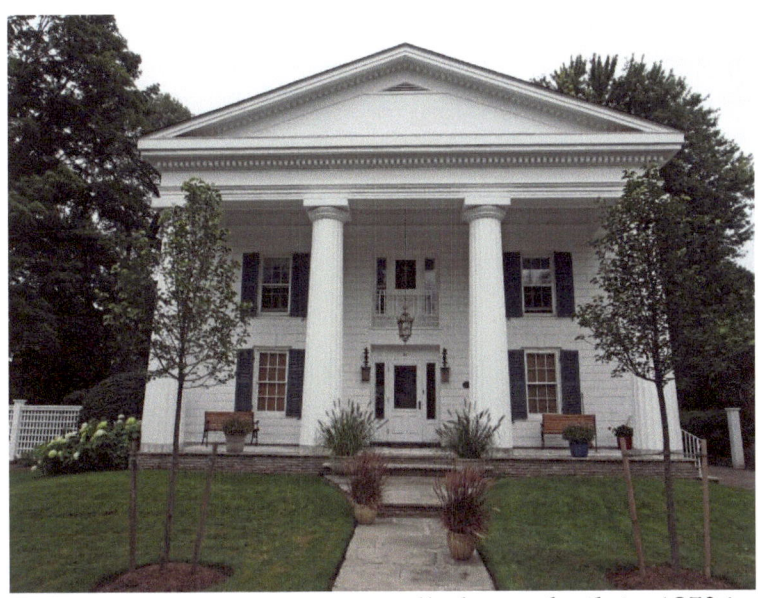

24 Pine Street – McLay-Minielly house built in 1853 in Classical Neo-Grecian (see Renaissance Revival style in appendix) architecture in frame construction of tongue and groove siding; entablature consisting of dentils, bands of moulding, frieze, and architrave;
two-storey-high Doric pillars, pediment

20 Pine Street – Italianate, cornice brackets

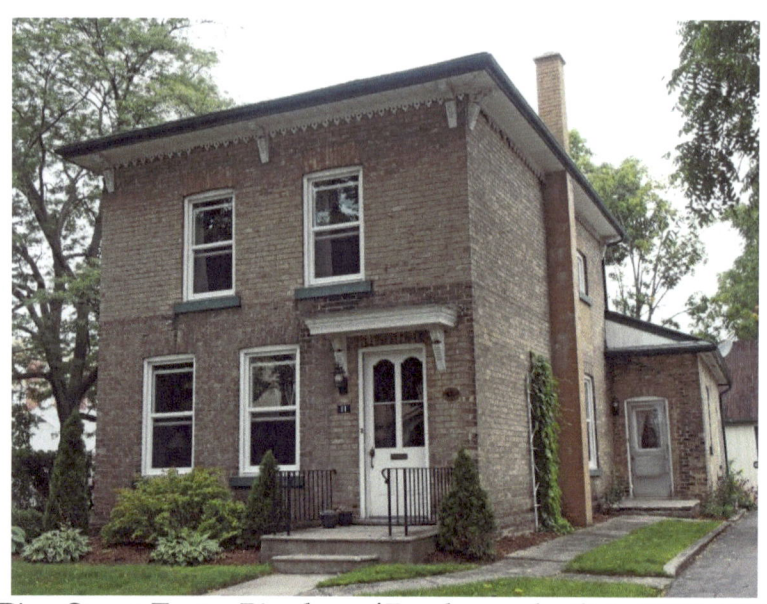

11 Pine Street East – Bingham/Foy house built in 1878-1879 of yellow brick in simple Italianate style, cornice brackets

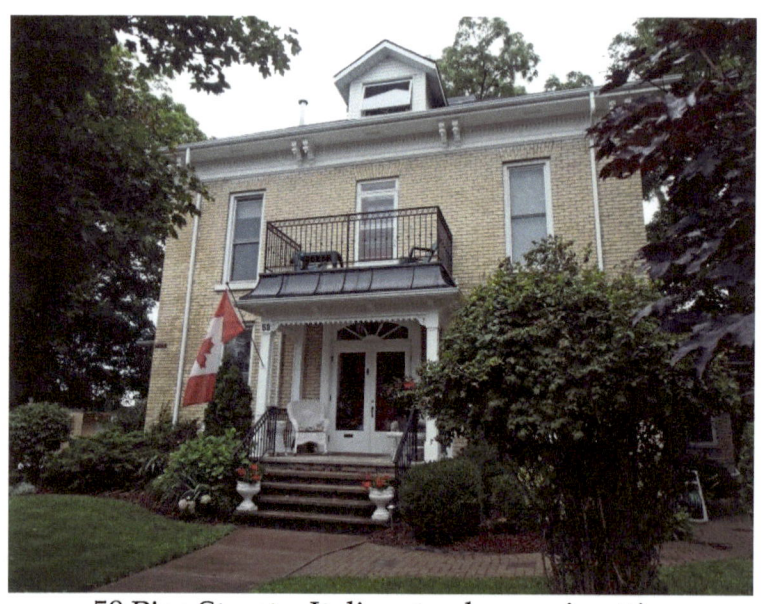

59 Pine Street – Italianate, dormer in attic, second-floor balcony

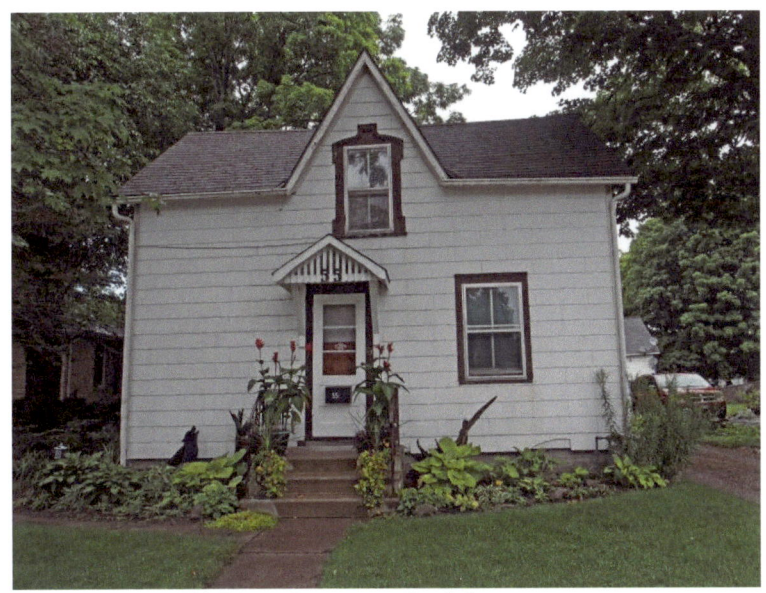

55 Pine Street – Gothic cottage

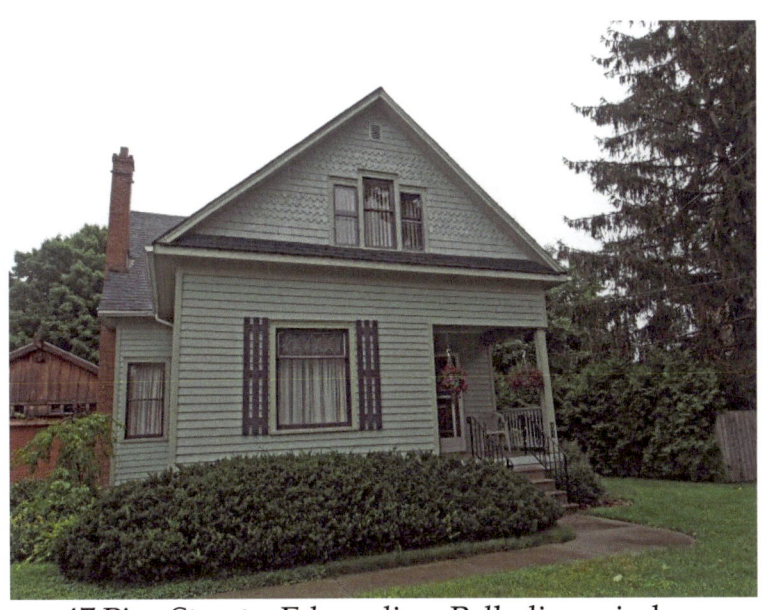

47 Pine Street – Edwardian, Palladian window

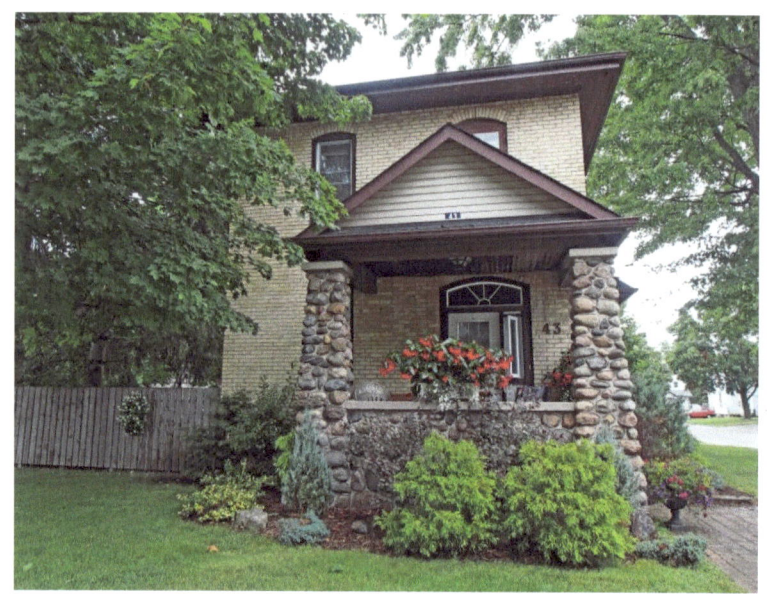

43 Pine Street – Italianate, pediment above porch

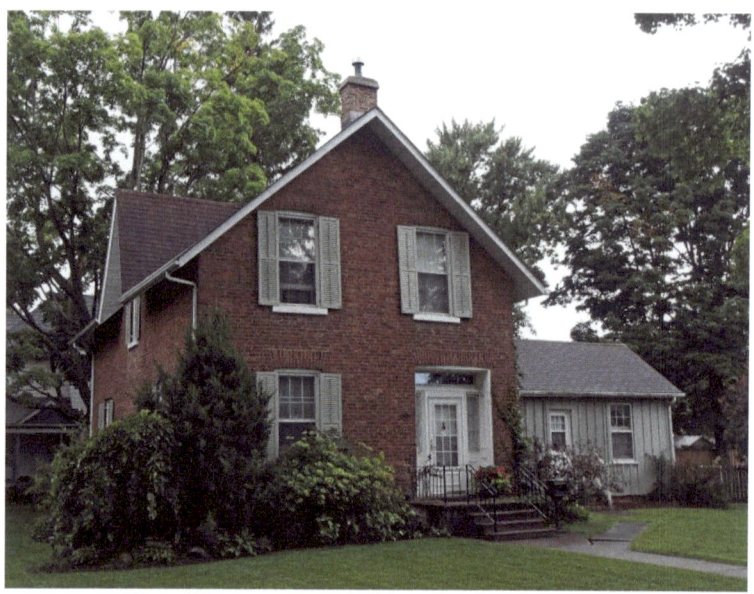

Pine Street – c. 1868 – Gothic Revival

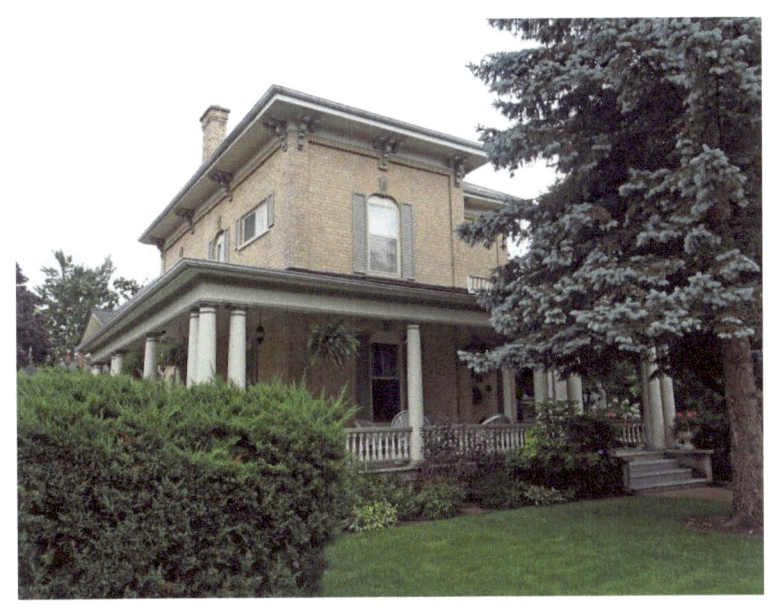

18 Pine Street – Italianate, cornice brackets, yellow brick, wraparound verandah

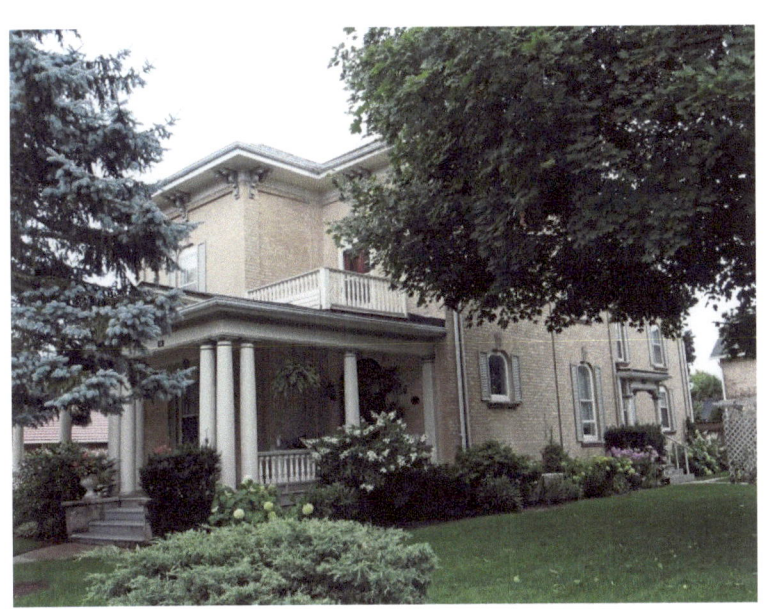

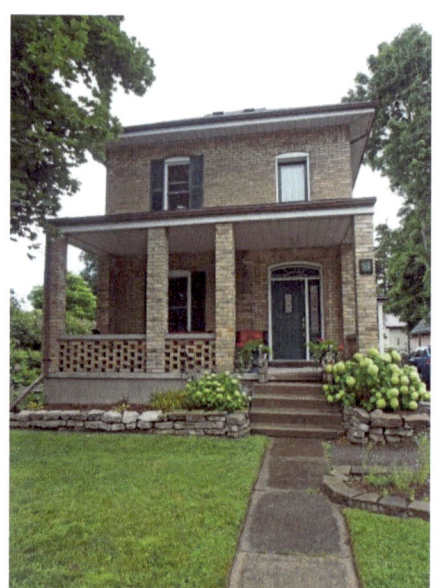

31 Pine Street - Italianate

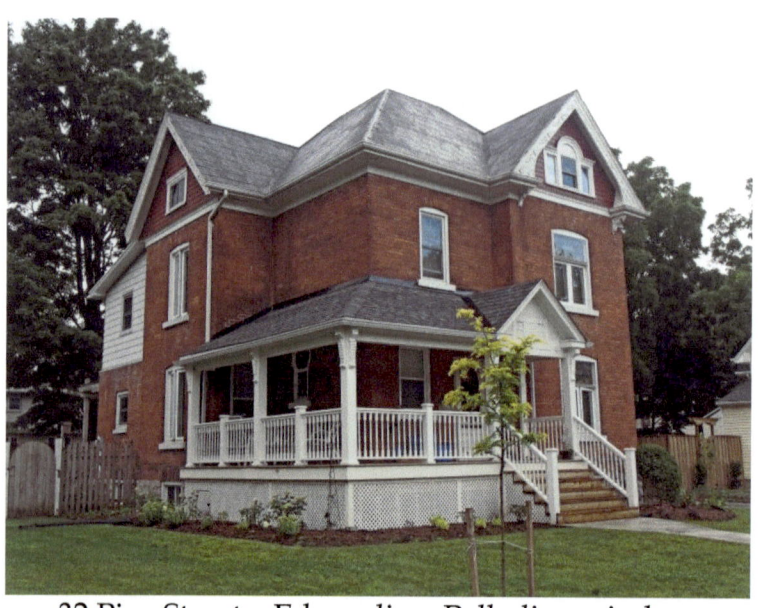

32 Pine Street – Edwardian, Palladian window

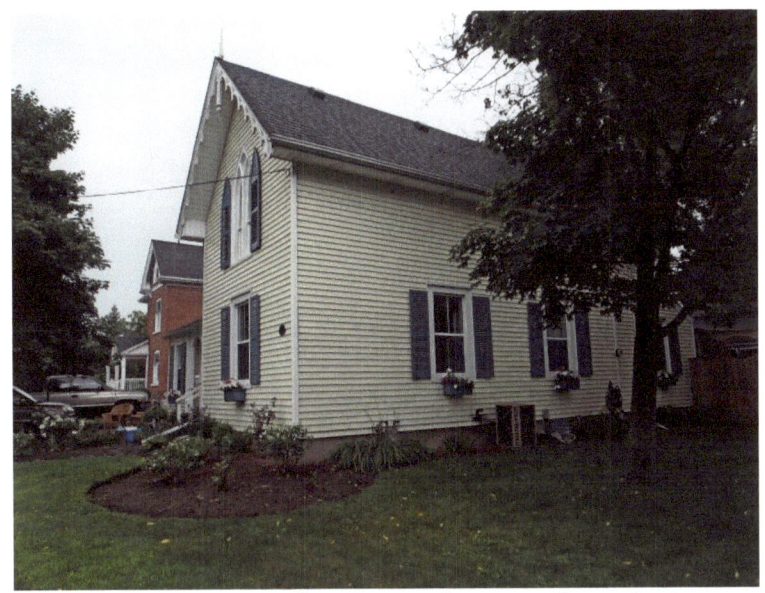

Pine Street – Gothic Revival – vergeboard trim

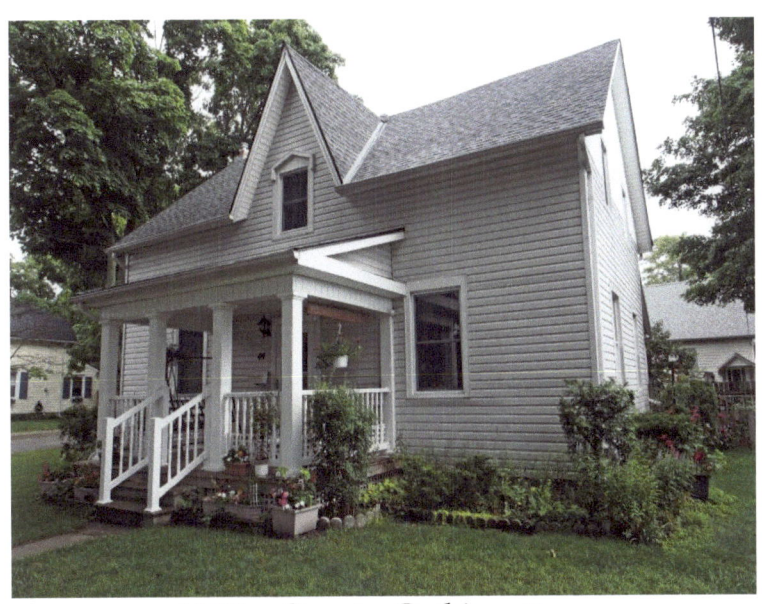

44 Pine Street – Gothic cottage

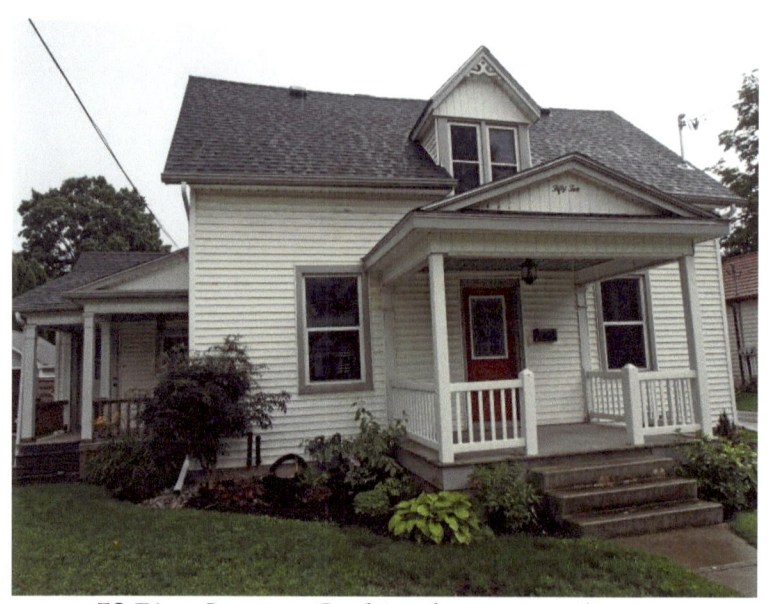

52 Pine Street – Gothic, dormer, pediment

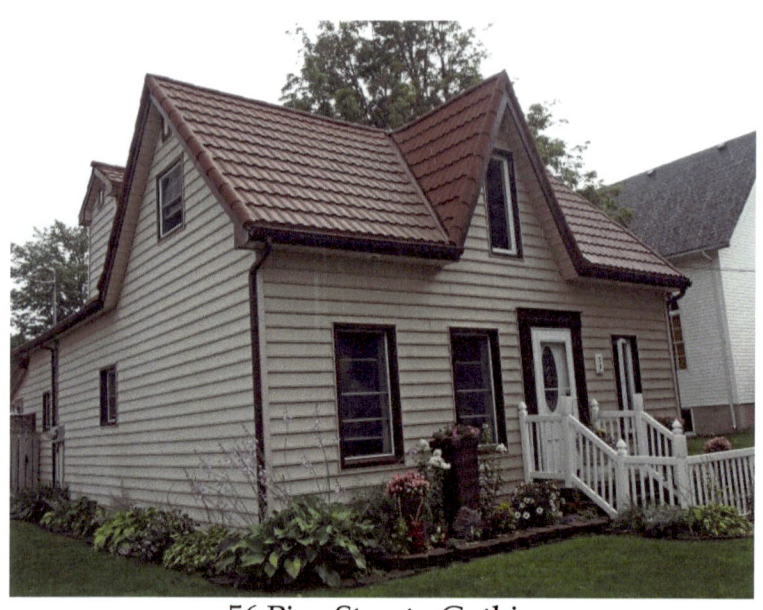

56 Pine Street - Gothic

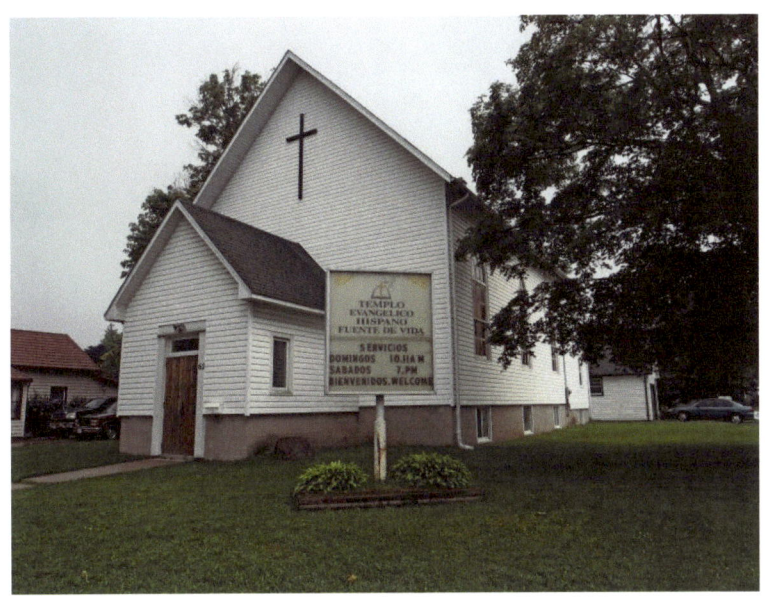

62 Pine Street – Templo Evangelico Hispano

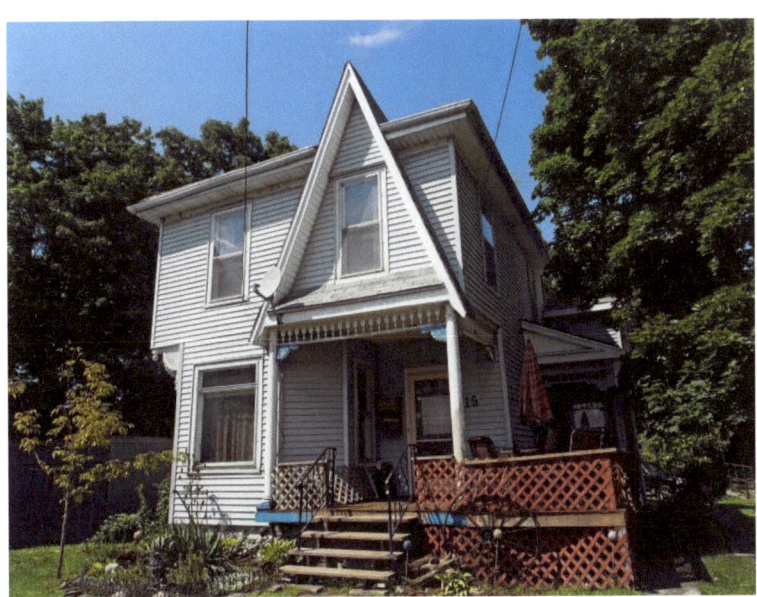

15 Water Street

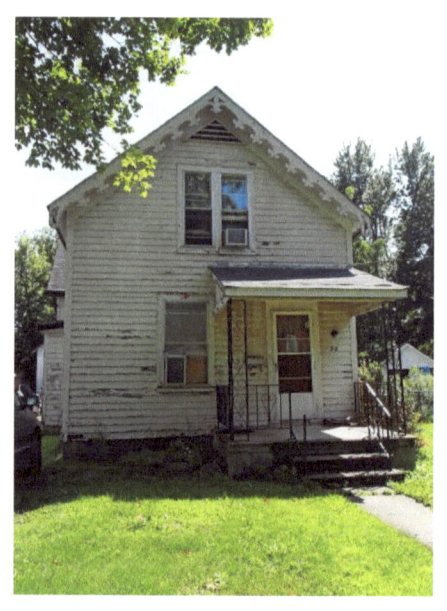

30 Water Street – Gothic, vergeboard trim on gable

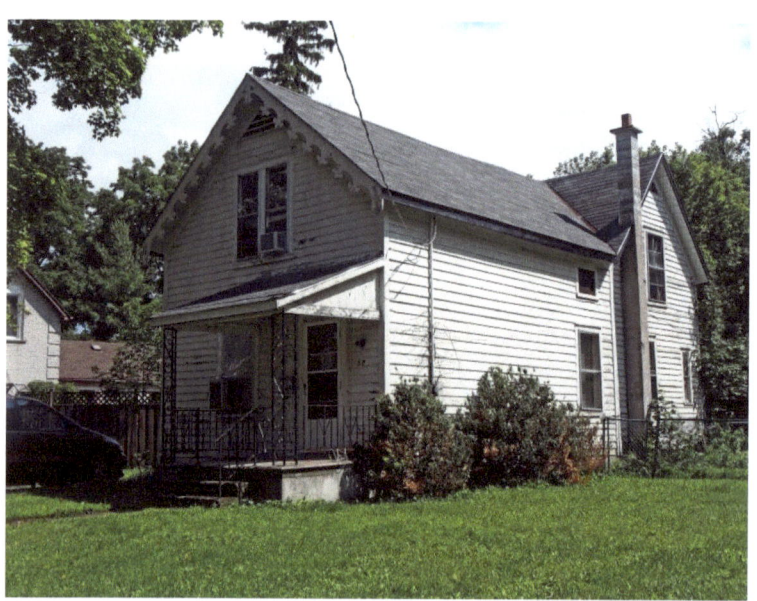

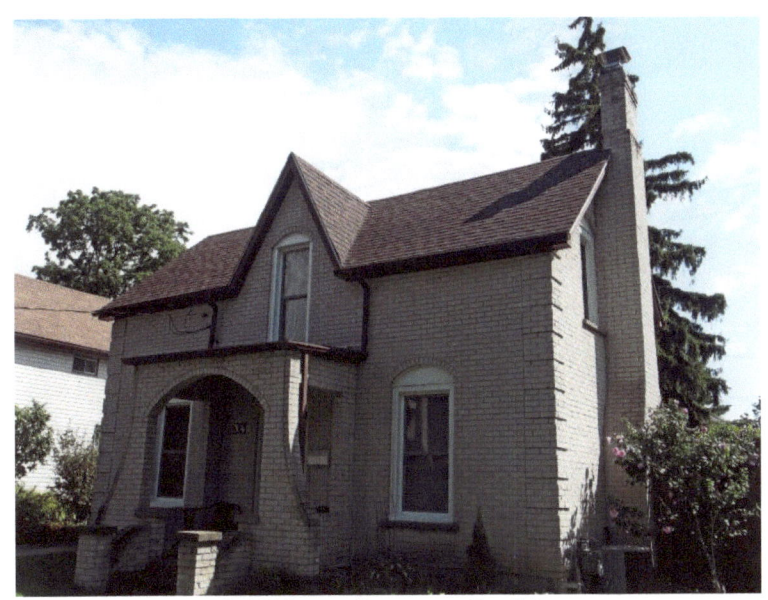

34 Water Street – Gothic

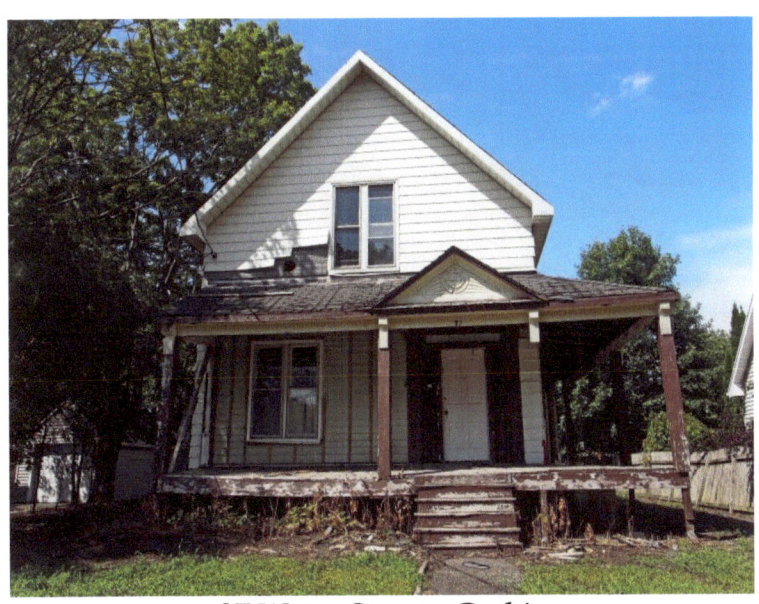

37 Water Street - Gothic

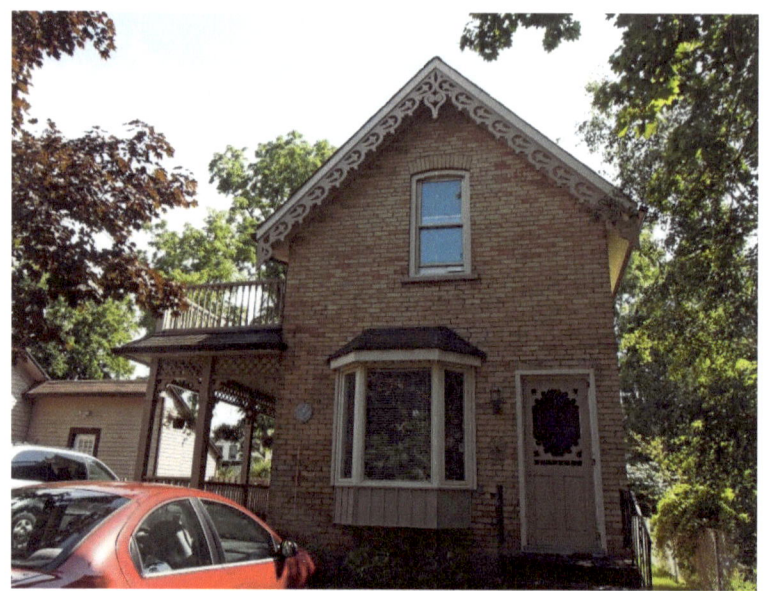

40 Water Street – Gothic Revival, vergeboard trim

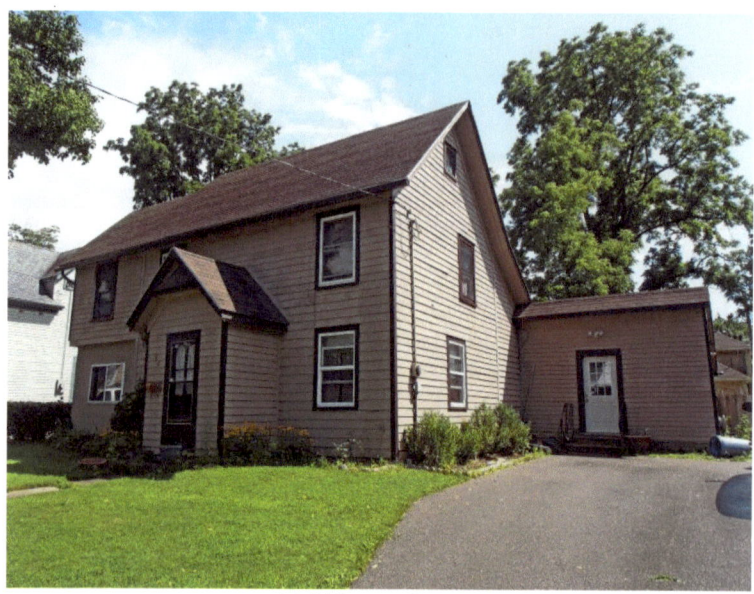

44 Water Street

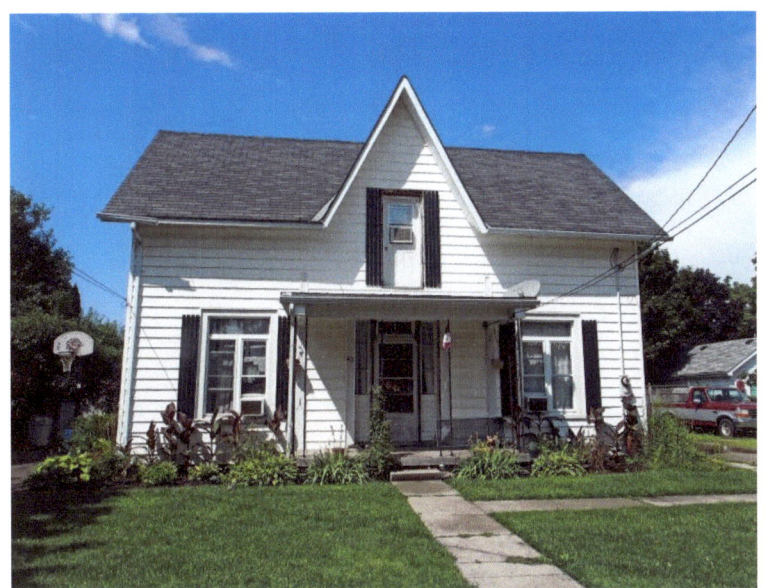

43 Water Street – Gothic cottage

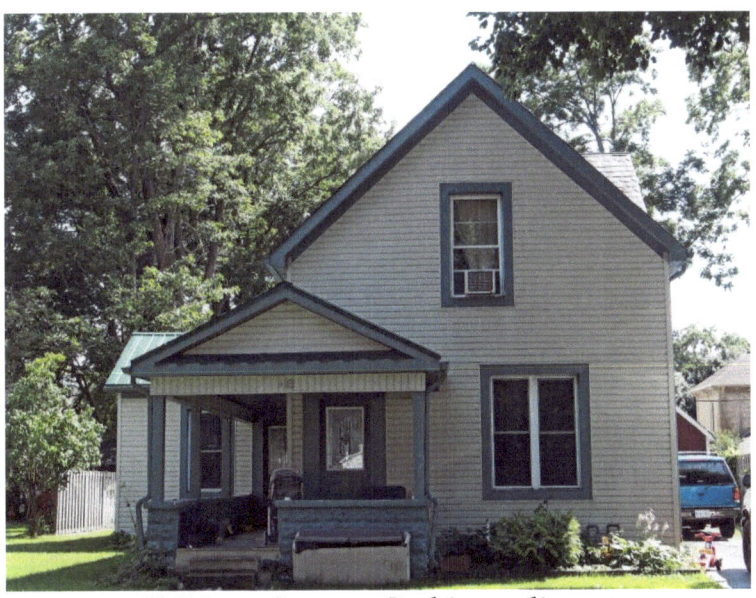

48 Water Street – Gothic, pediment

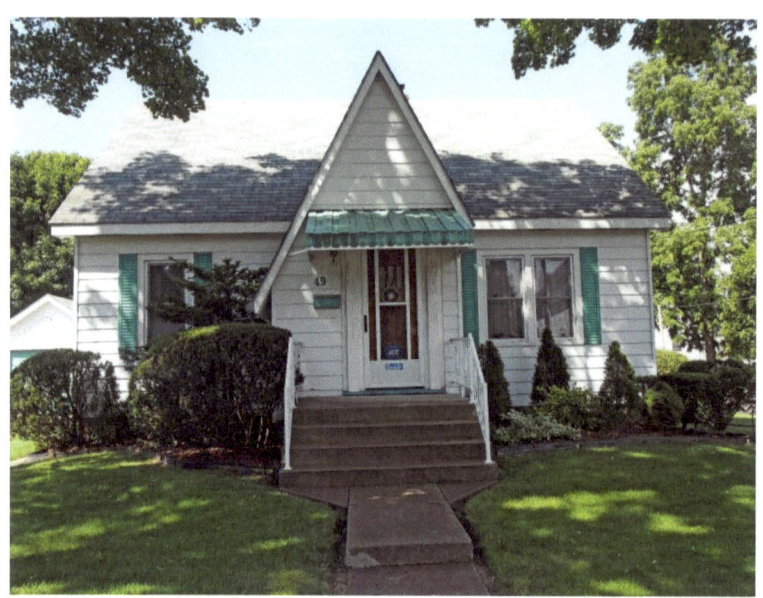

49 Water Street – Gothic cottage

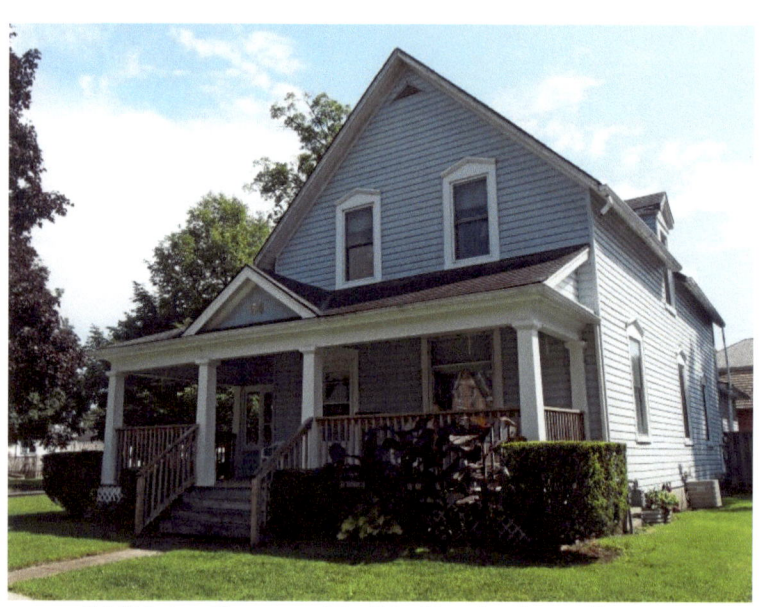

54 Water Street – Gothic Revival, pediment

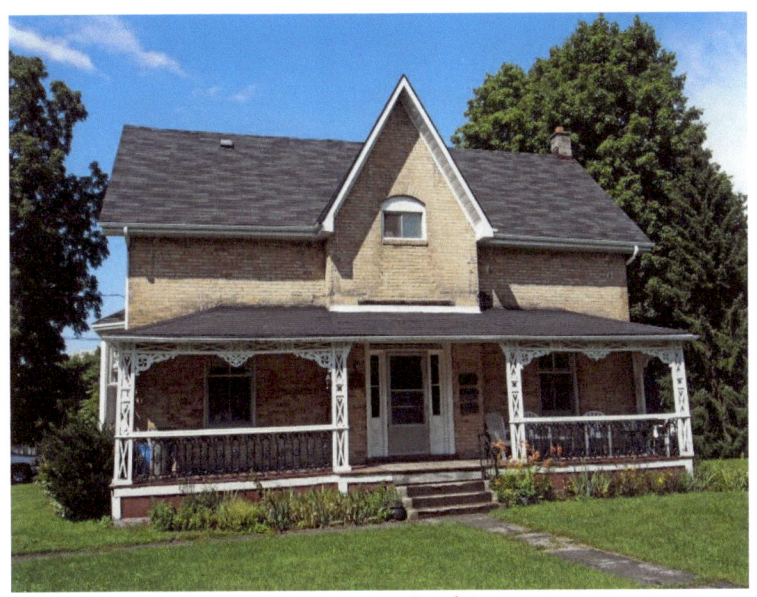

57 Water Street – Gothic cottage

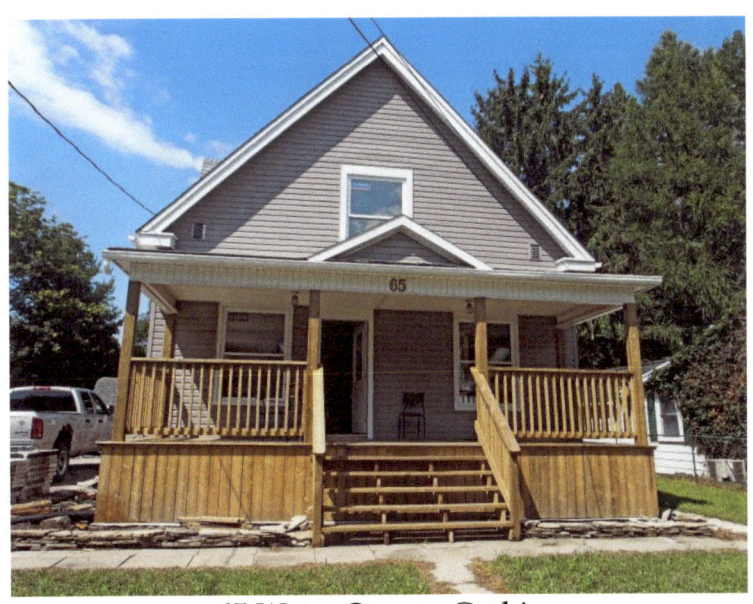

65 Water Street - Gothic

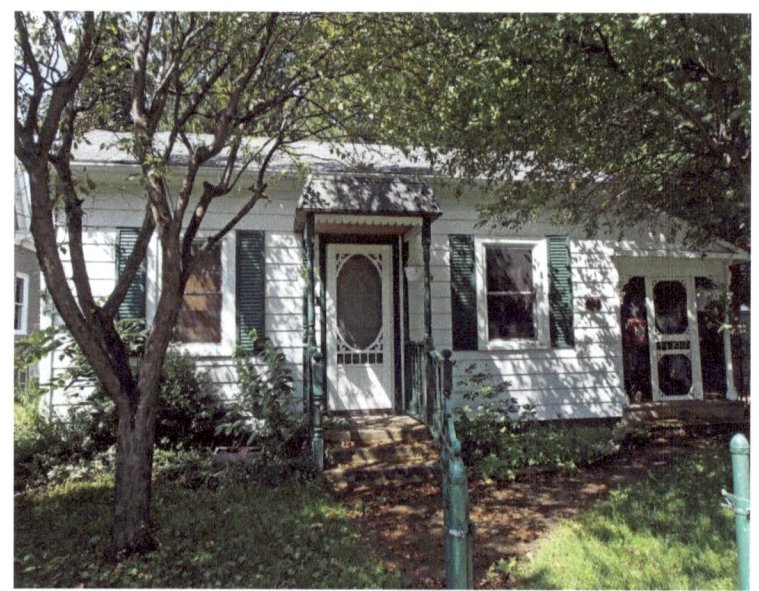

67 Water Street

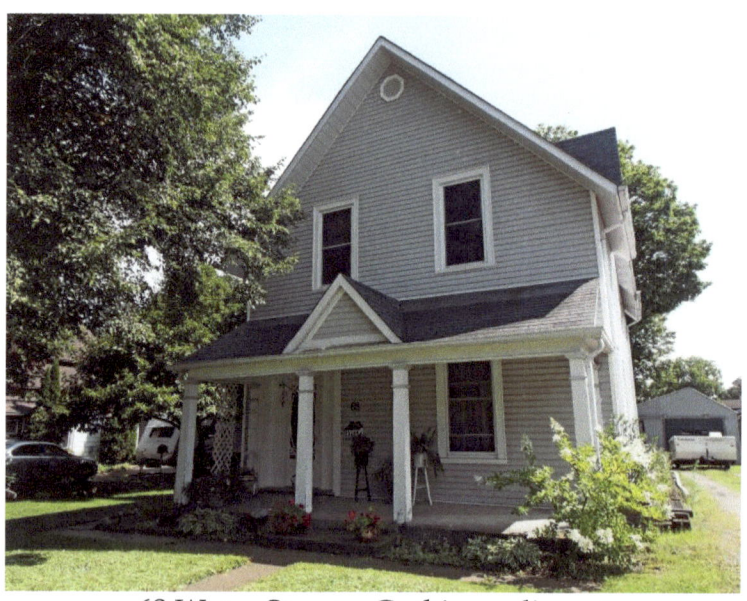

68 Water Street – Gothic, pediment

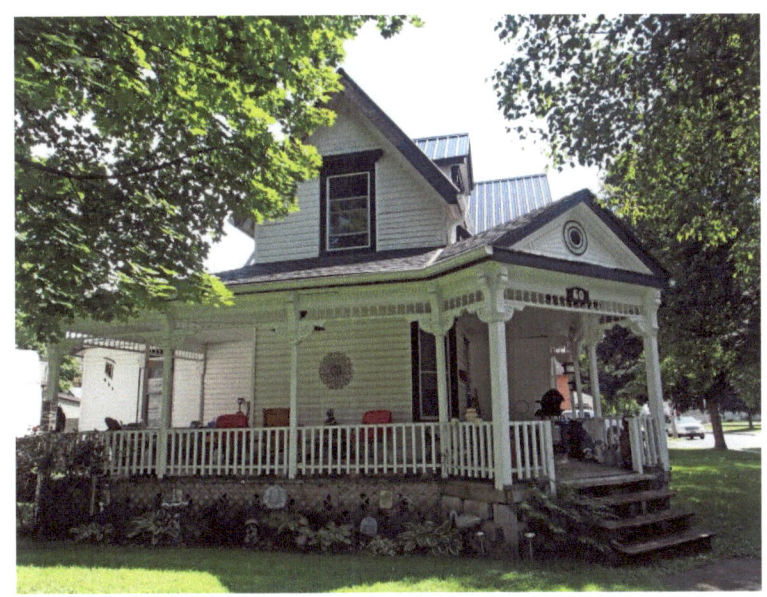

60 Water Street – Gothic Revival,
pediment with decorated tympanum

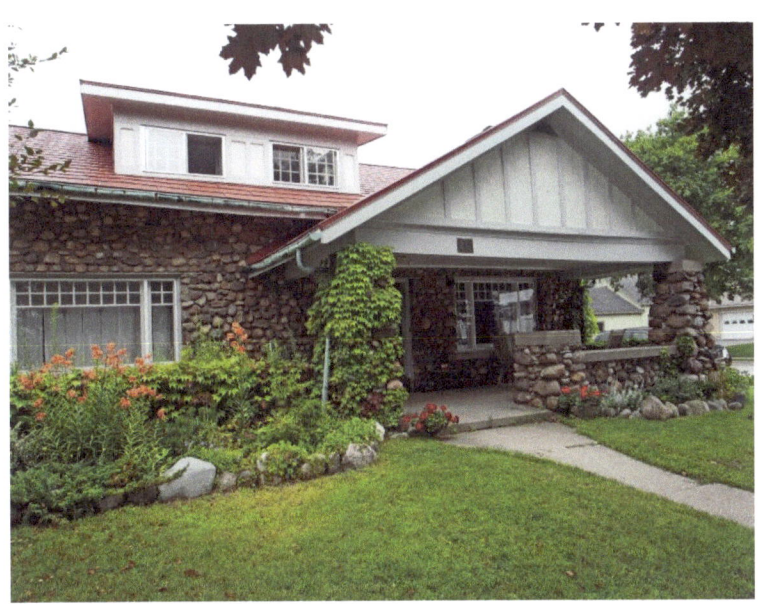

8 Sydenham Street East, dormer

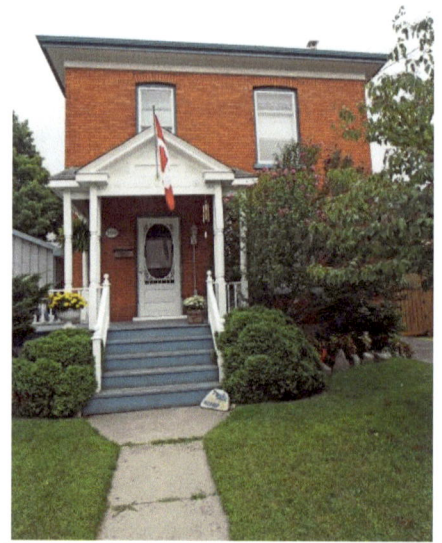

100 Sydenham Street East - Italianate

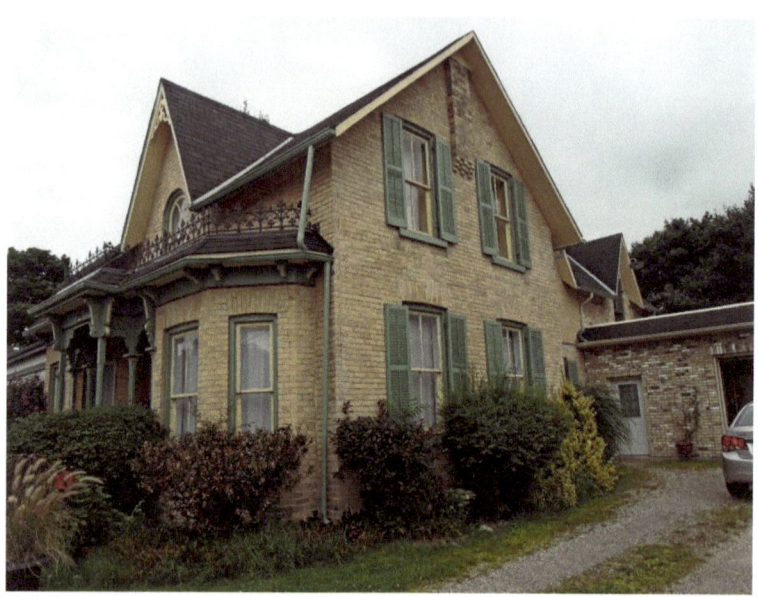

116 Sydenham Street East – Gothic Revival, iron cresting above bay window and porch

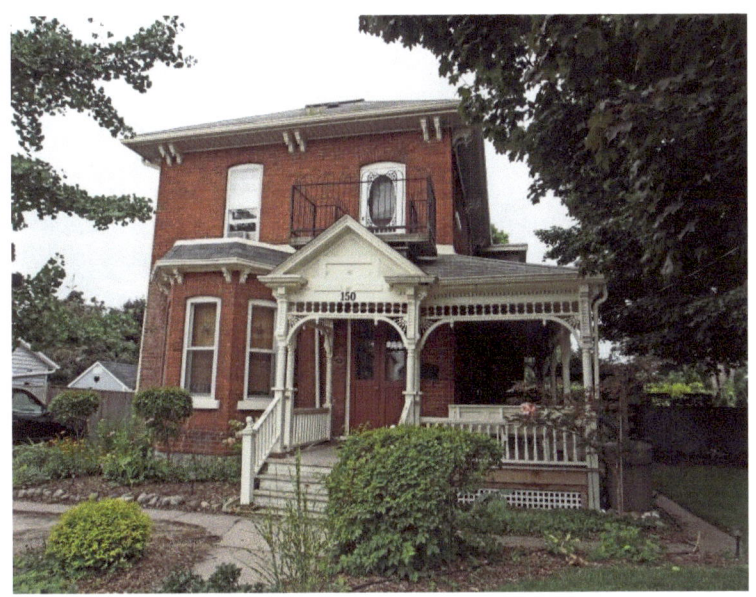

150 Sydenham Street East – Italianate, paired cornice brackets, bay window, wraparound porch

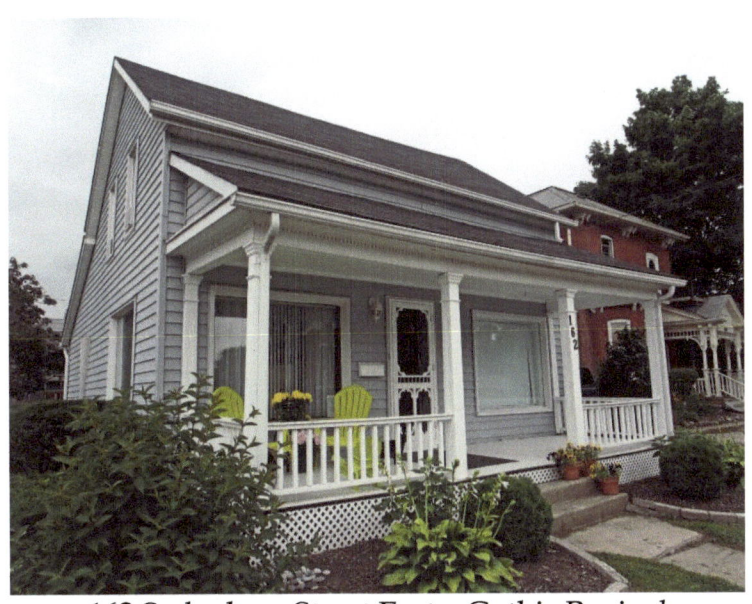

162 Sydenham Street East – Gothic Revival

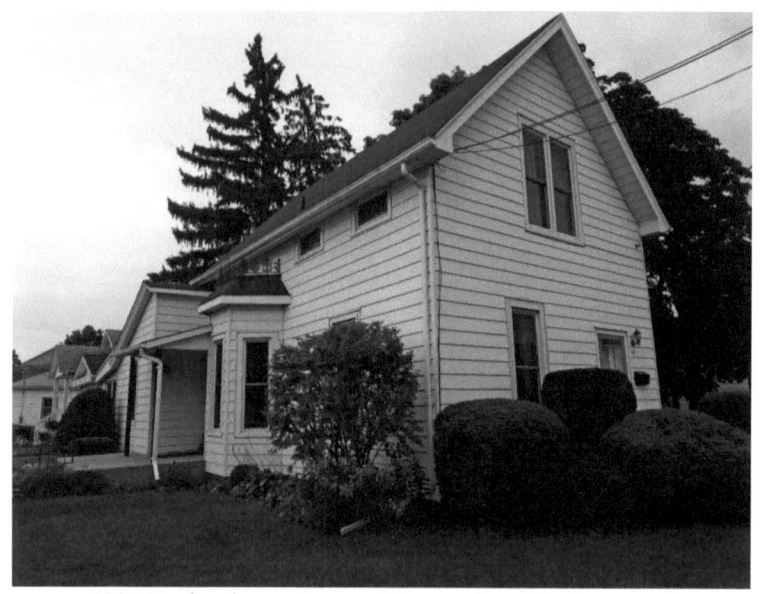

174 Sydenham Street East – Gothic Revival

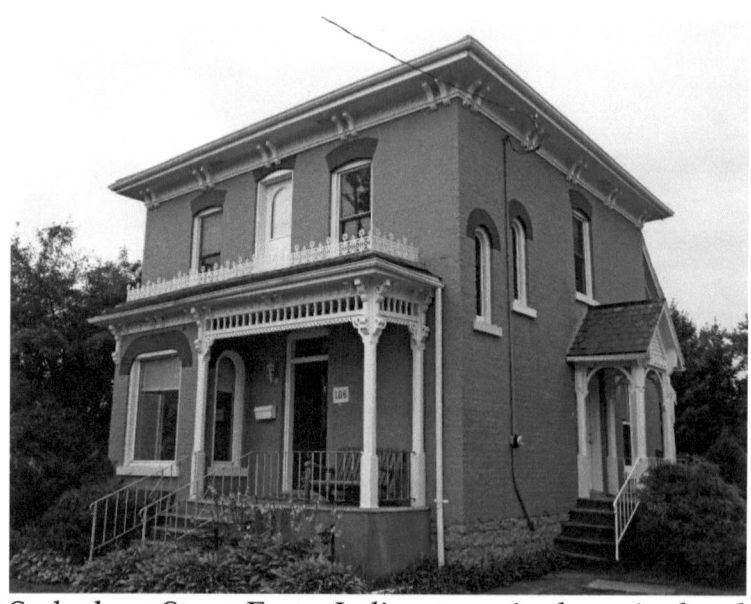

186 Sydenham Street East – Italianate, paired cornice brackets, iron cresting around second floor

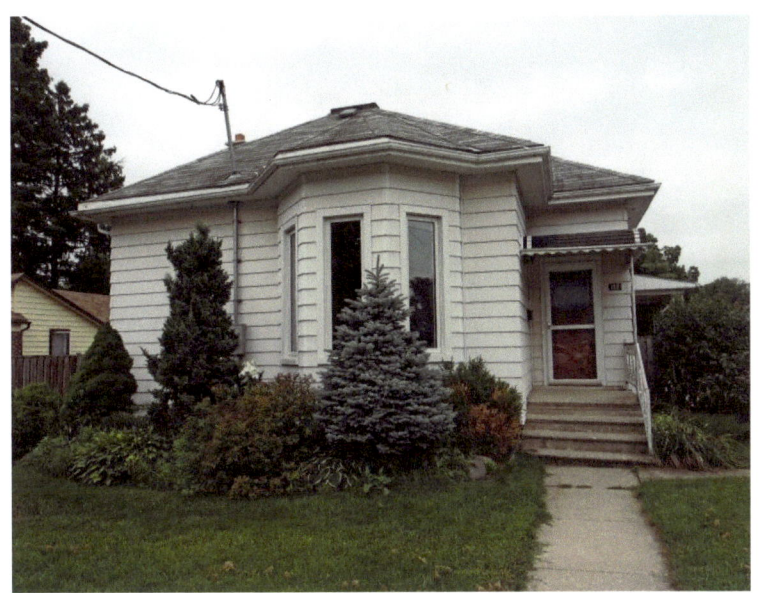

192 Sydenham Street East – cottage, hipped roof

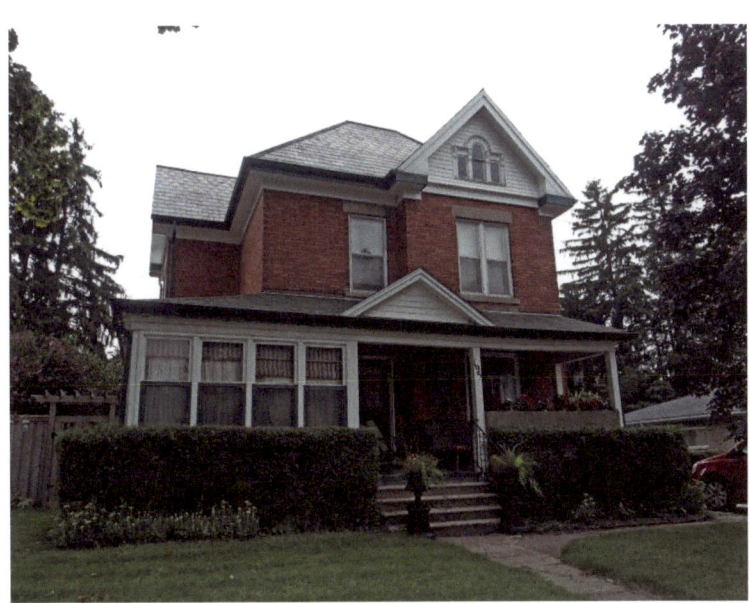

195 Sydenham Street East – Edwardian – Palladian window, pediment

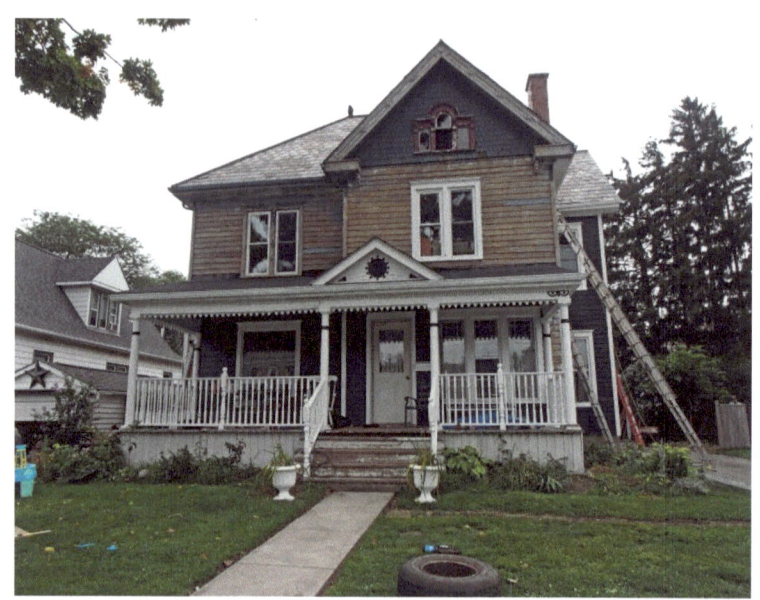

Sydenham Street East – Edwardian, Palladian window,
Pediment with decorated tympanum

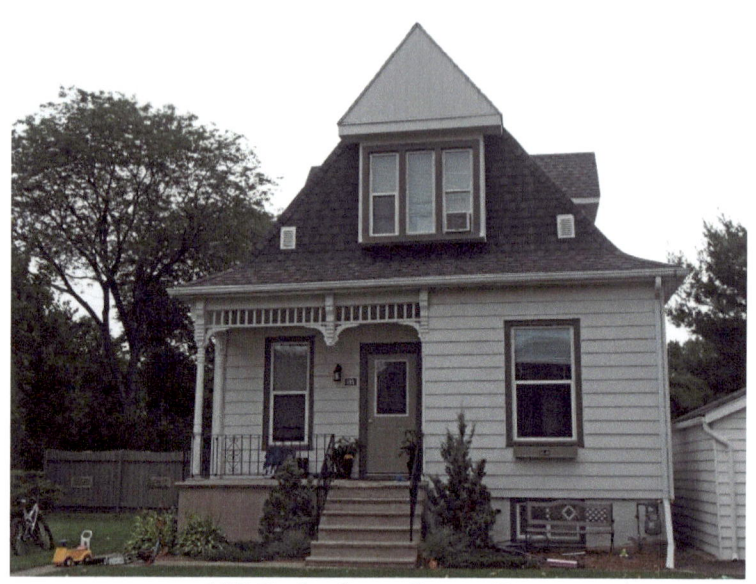

185 Sydenham Street East

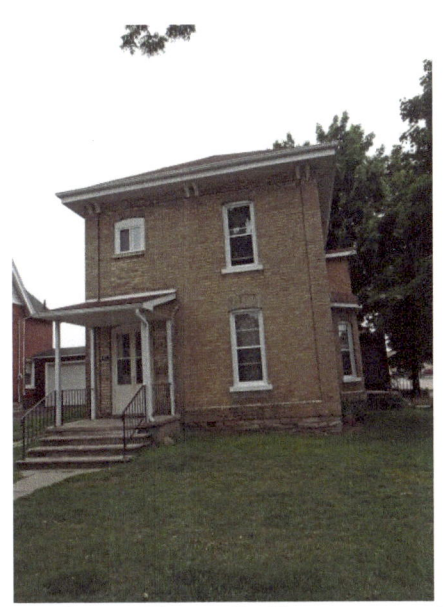

157 Sydenham Street East – Italianate, cornice brackets

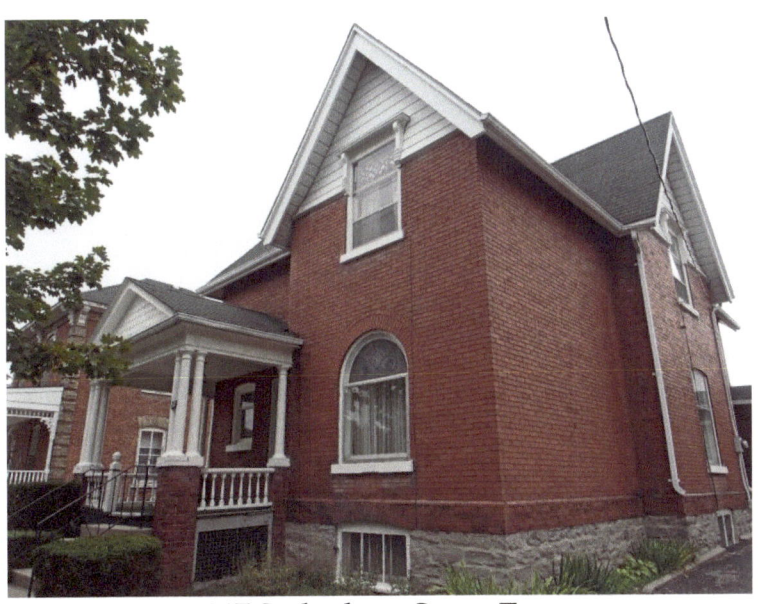

147 Sydenham Street East

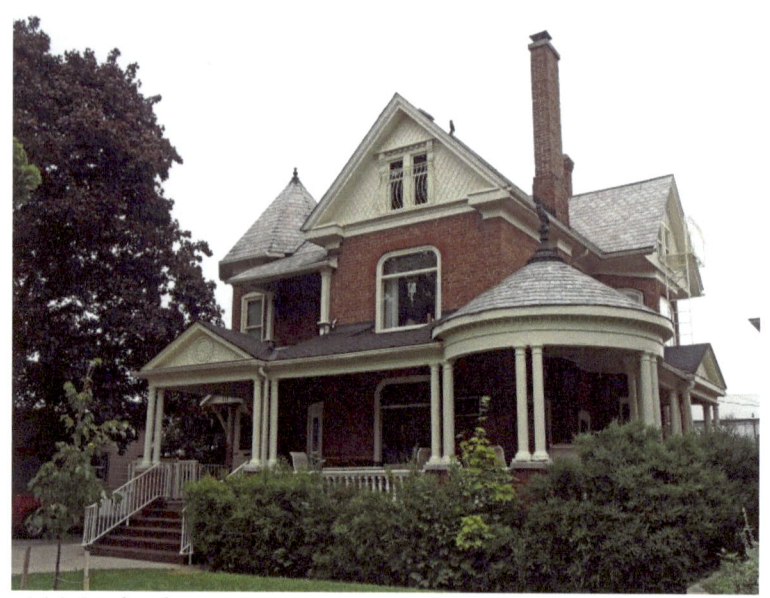

111 Sydenham Street East – Queen Anne style, turret

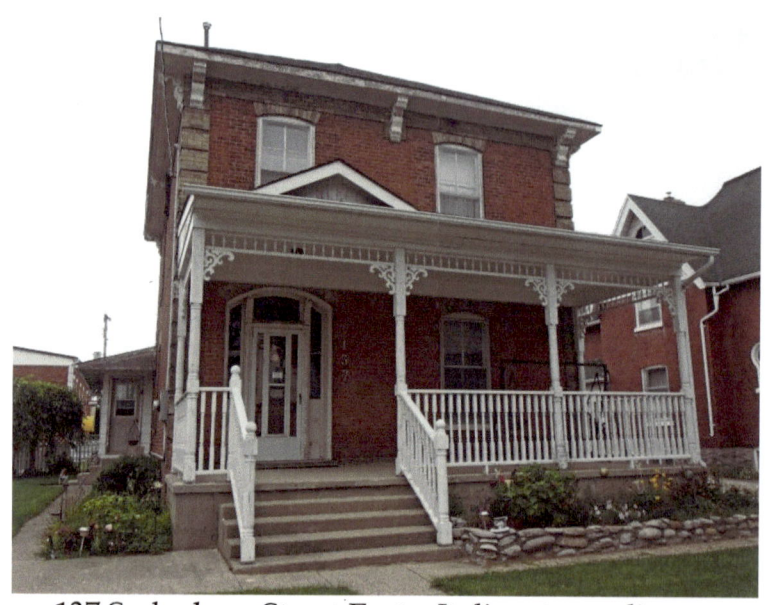

137 Sydenham Street East – Italianate, pediment

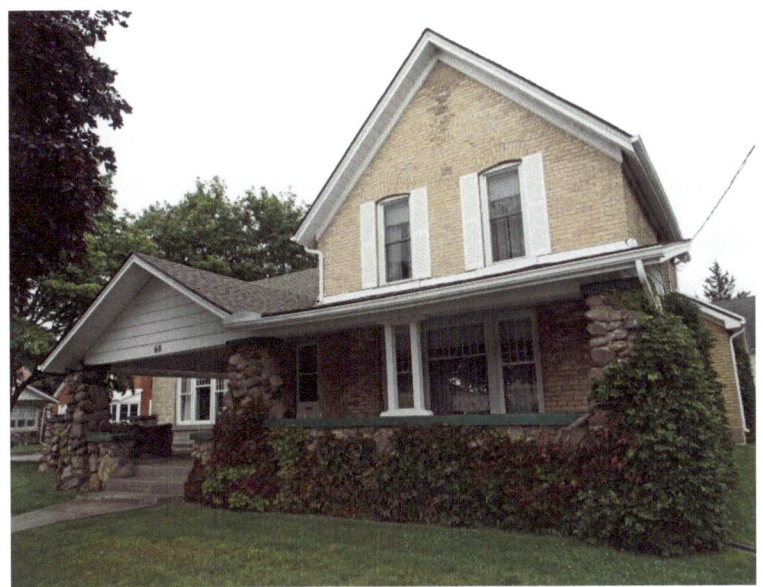

60 Sydenham Street East – Gothic Revival

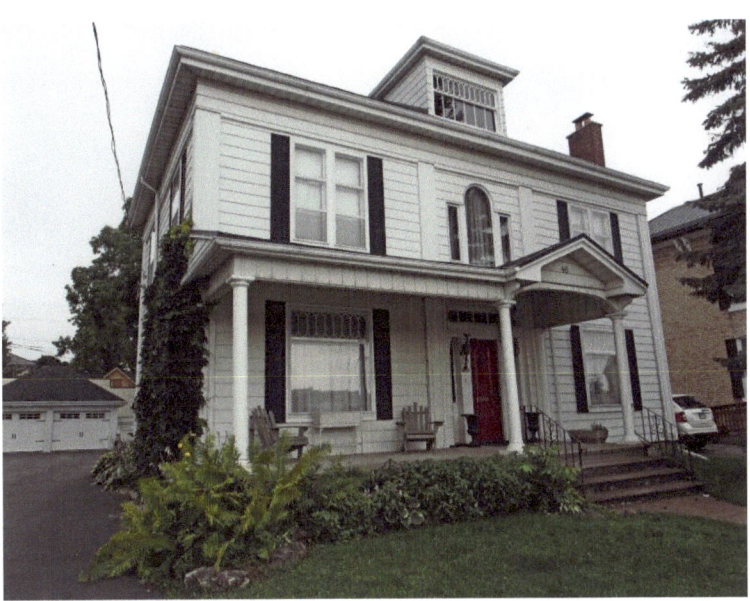

46 Sydenham Street East – Italianate, dormer, pediment

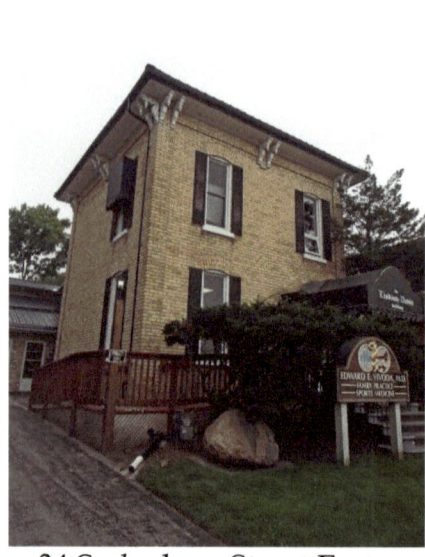

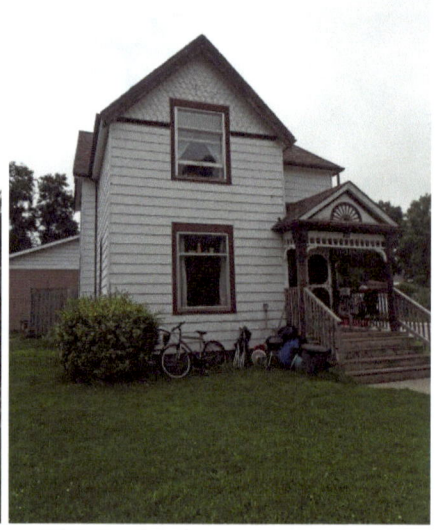

34 Sydenham Street East
Italianate, cornice brackets

124 Sydenham Street East
Gothic Revival, pediment
With decorated tympanum

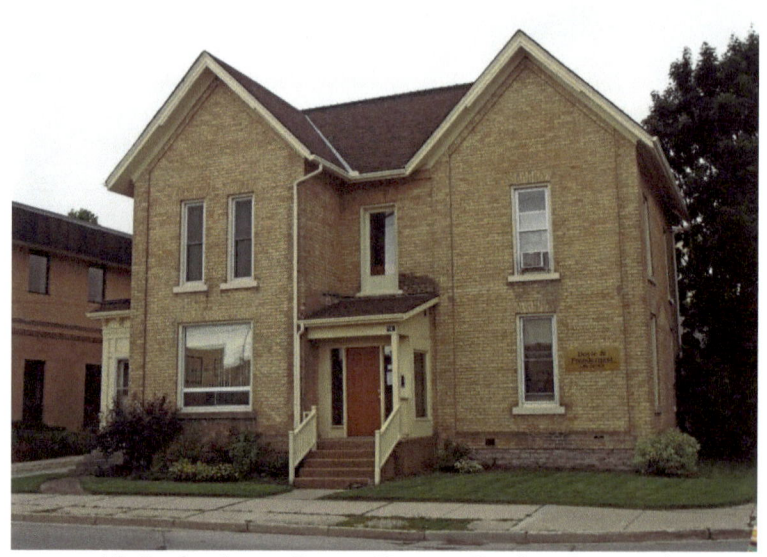

10 Sydenham Street East – Gothic Revival

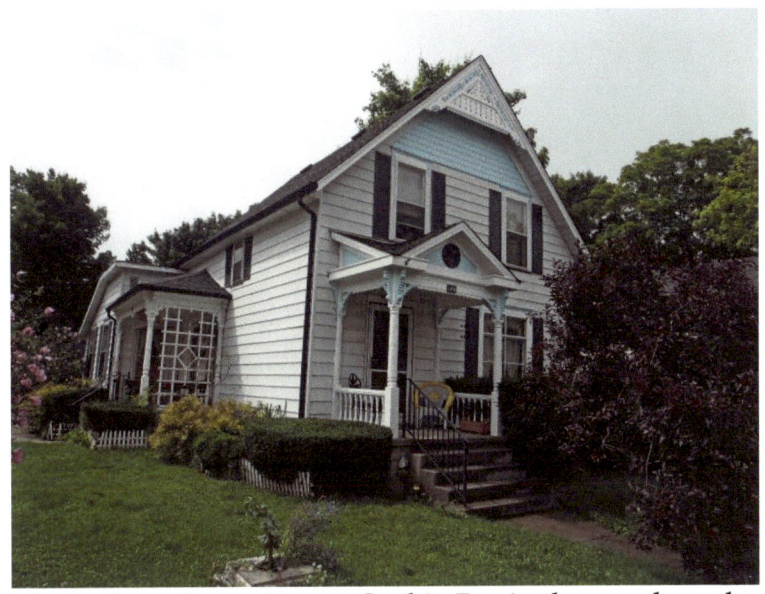

144 Sydenham Street East – Gothic Revival, vergeboard trim
on gable, pediment above porch with decorated tympanum

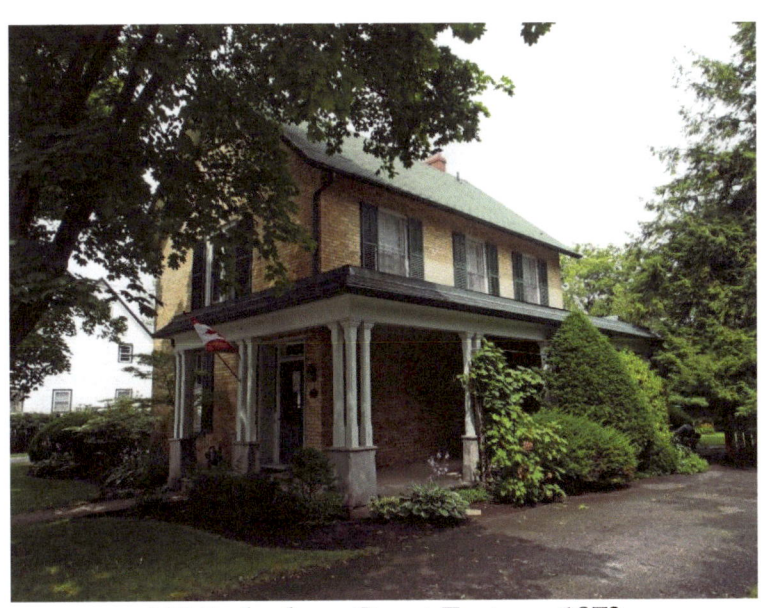

103 Sydenham Street East – c. 1873

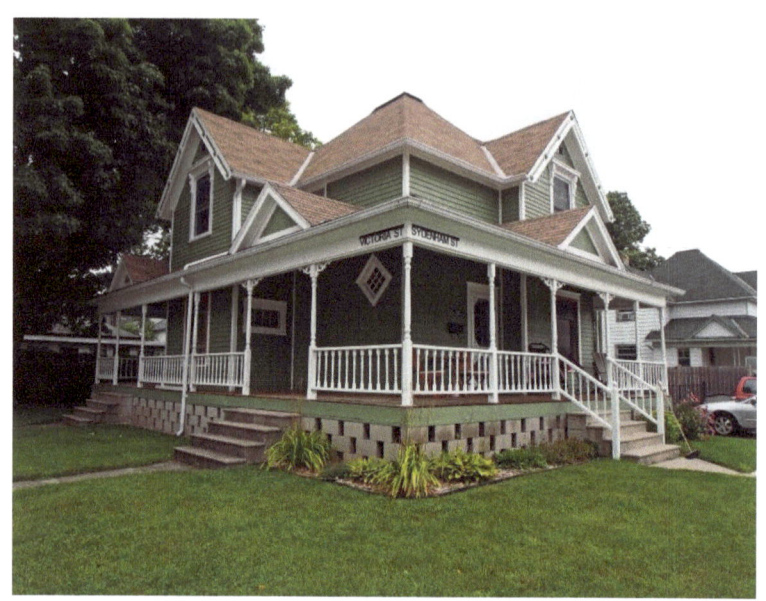

235 Sydenham Street East

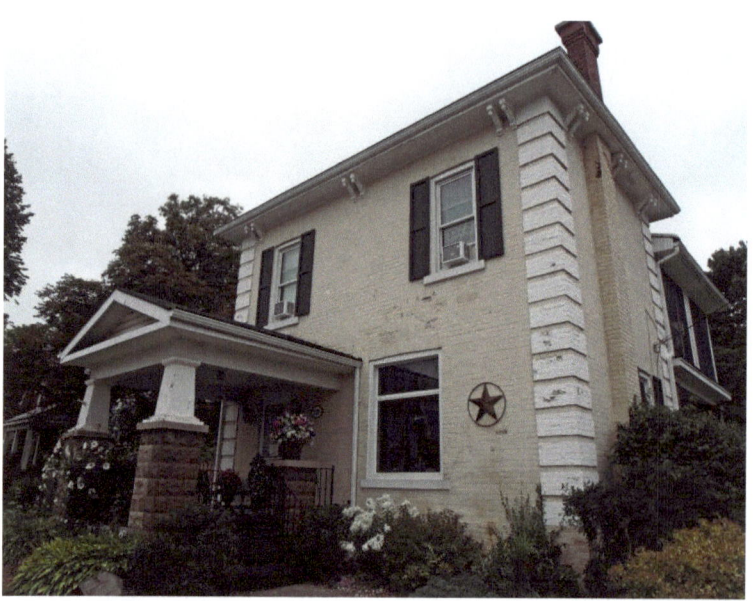

319 Sydenham Street East – Italianate, corner quoins, cornice brackets, pediment above porch

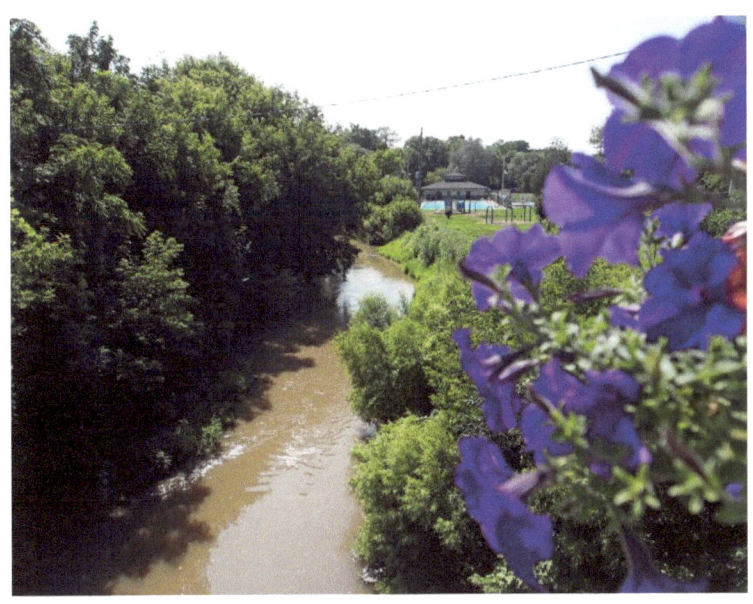

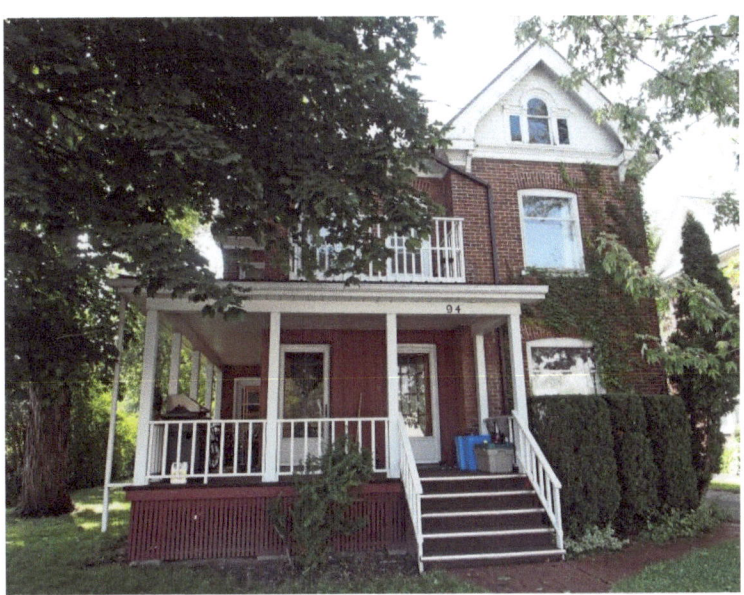

94 John Street North – Edwardian, Palladian window,
Balcony on second floor, wrap-around verandah

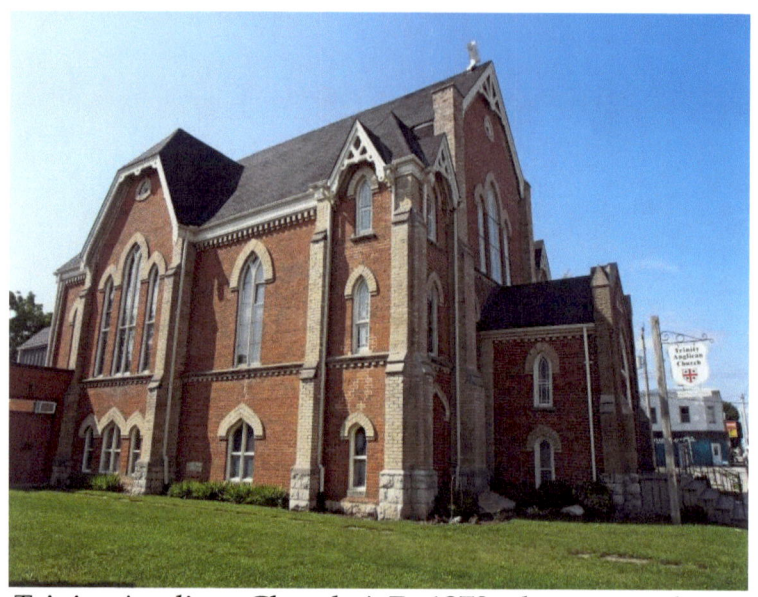

Trinity Anglican Church A.D. 1879 – lancet windows, buttresses, dentil moulding, dichromatic brickwork

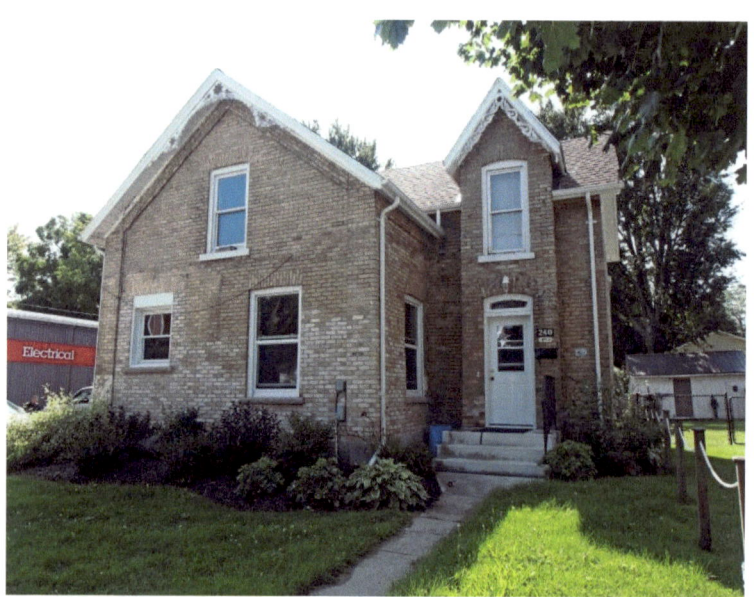

240 John Street North – Gothic Revival, vergeboard trim on gables, yellow brick

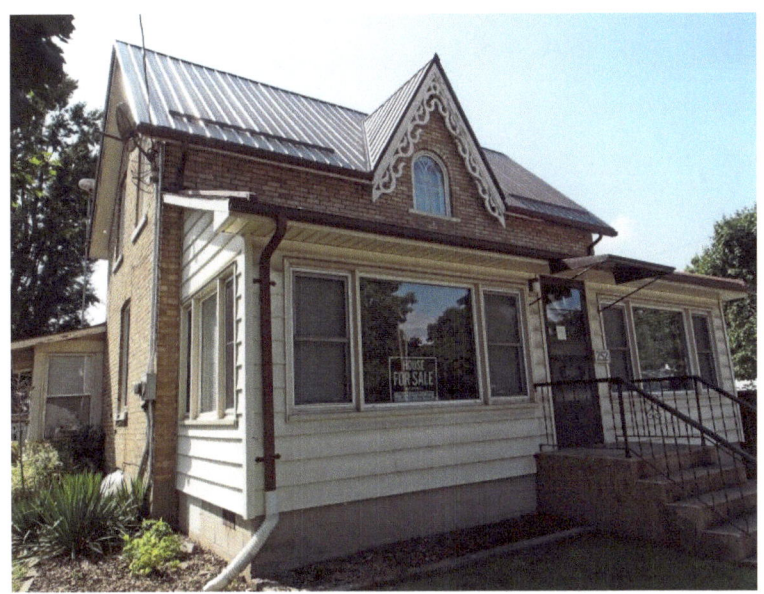

252 John Street North – Gothic cottage, vergeboard trim

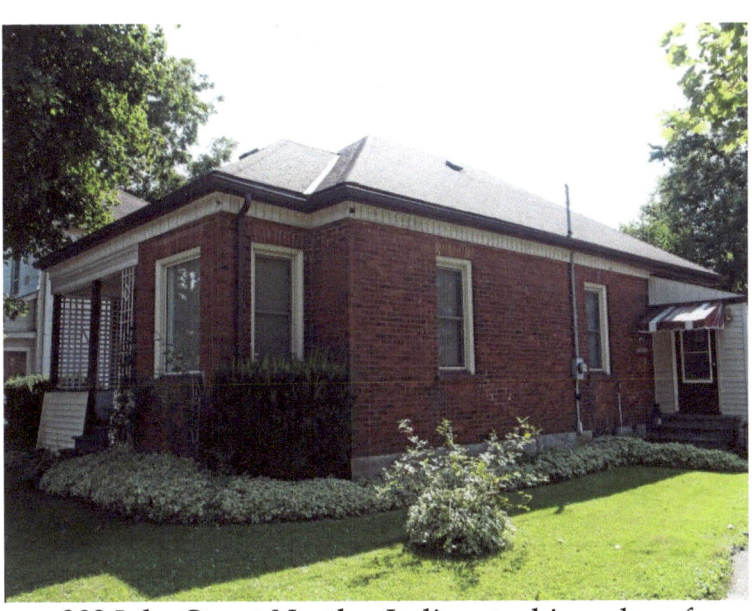

302 John Street North – Italianate, hipped roof

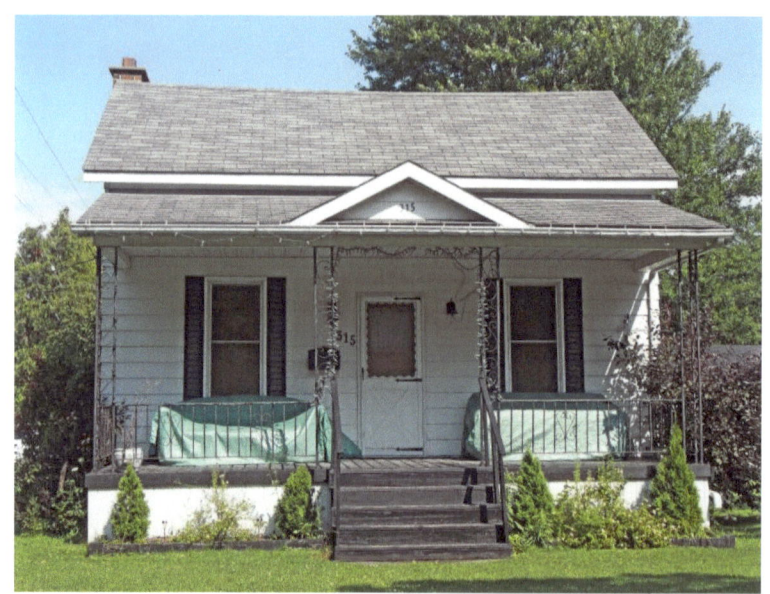

315 John Street North

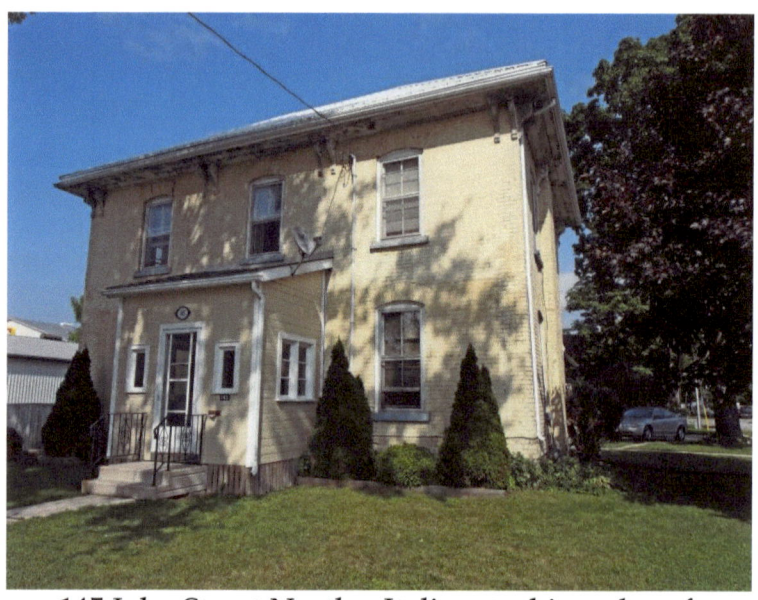

145 John Street North – Italianate, hipped roof,
Paired cornice brackets

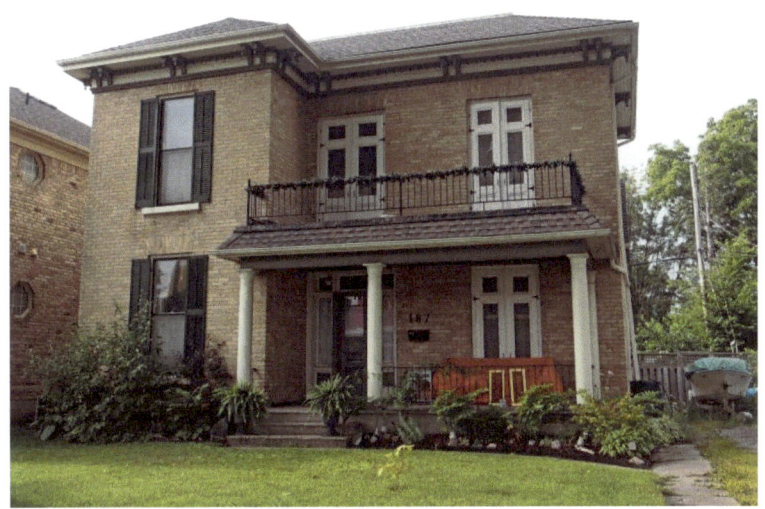

187 John Street North – Italianate, paired cornice brackets, balcony on second floor, hipped roof

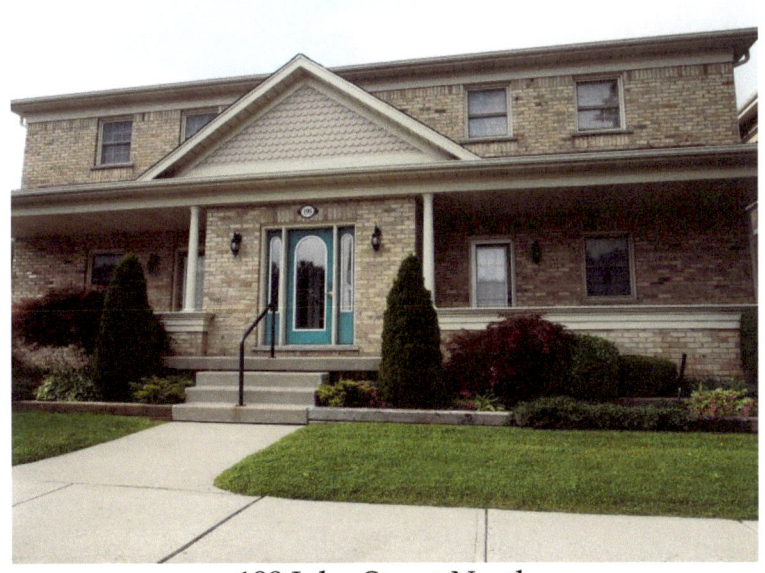

199 John Street North

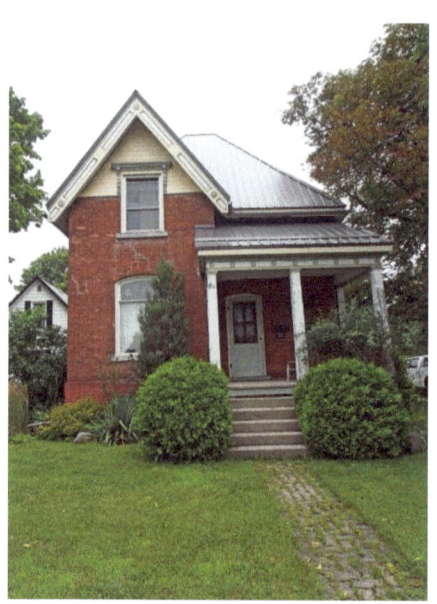

313 Talbot Street East

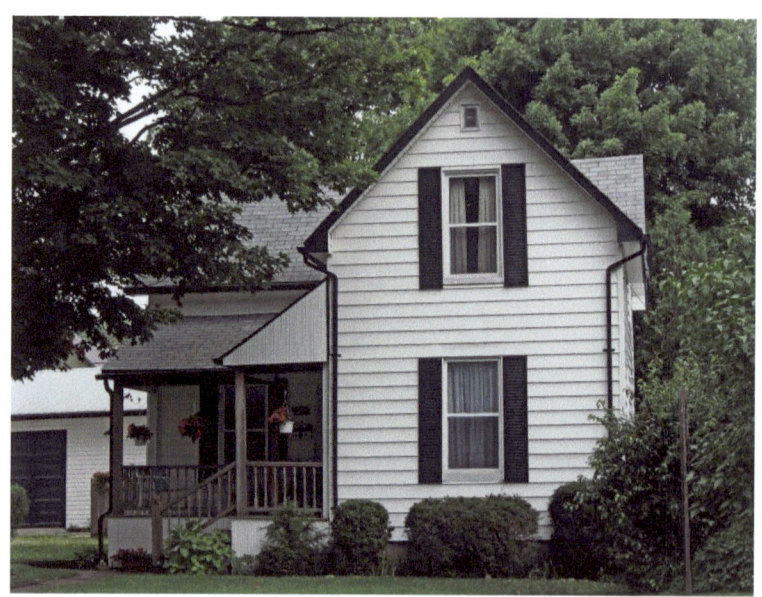

311 Talbot Street East

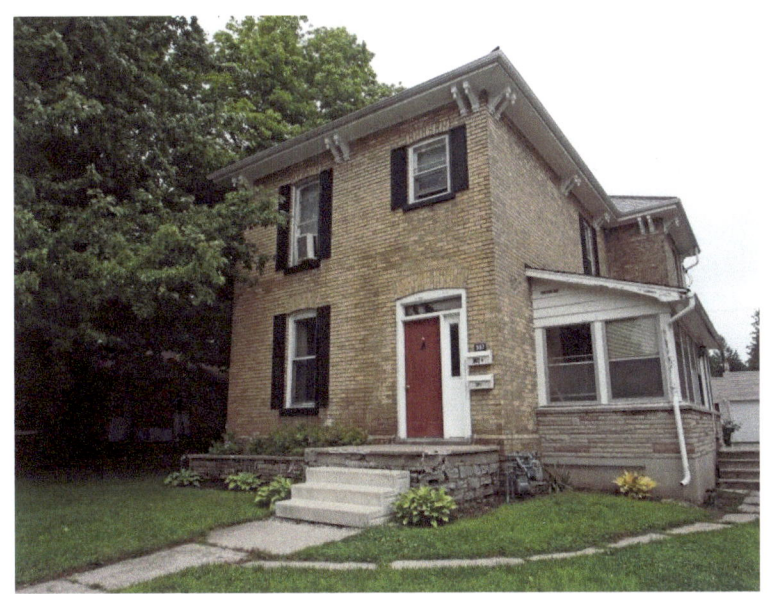

307 Talbot Street East – Italianate, paired cornice brackets

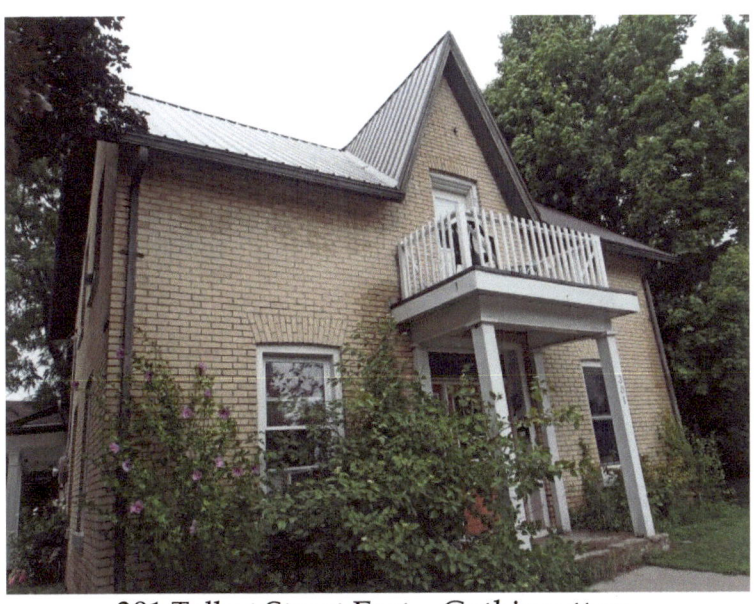

301 Talbot Street East – Gothic cottage

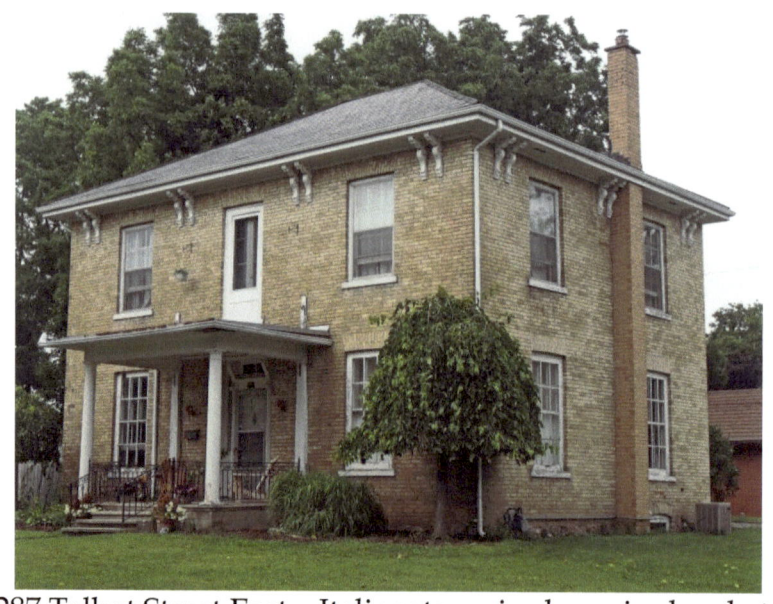

287 Talbot Street East – Italianate, paired cornice brackets

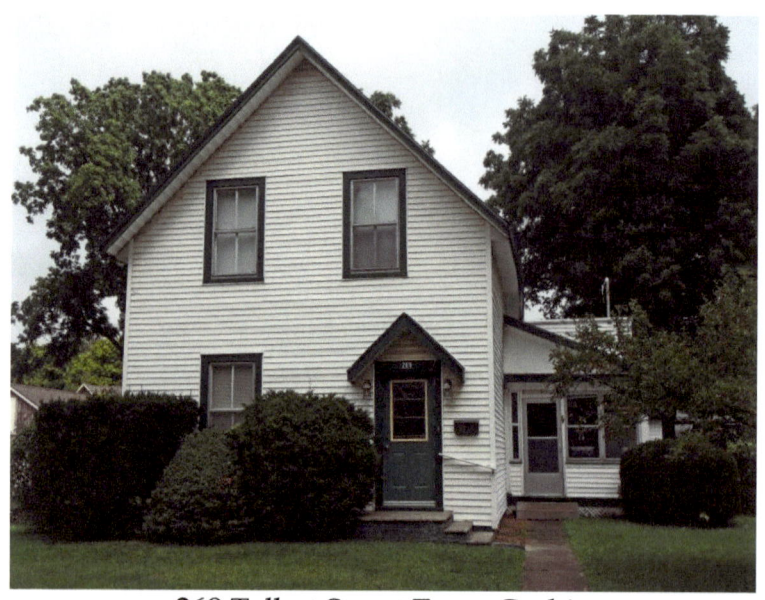

269 Talbot Street East - Gothic

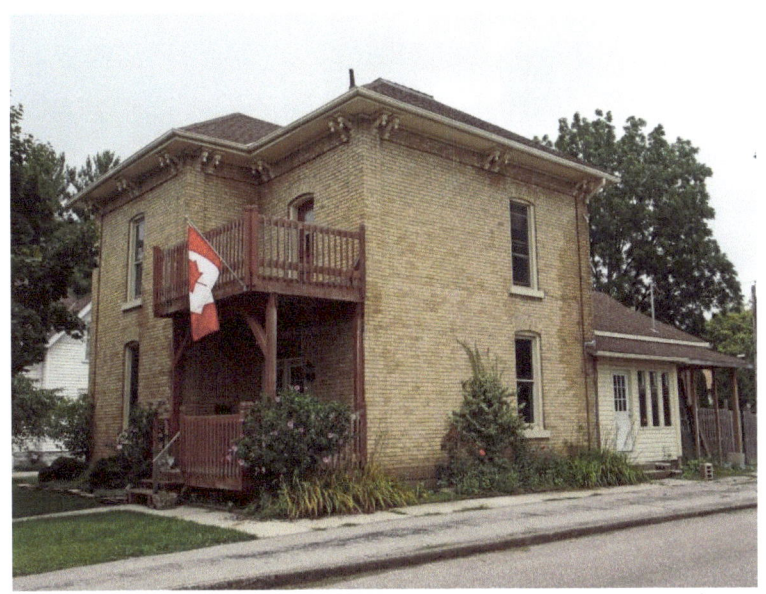

Talbot Street East – Italianate, paired cornice brackets

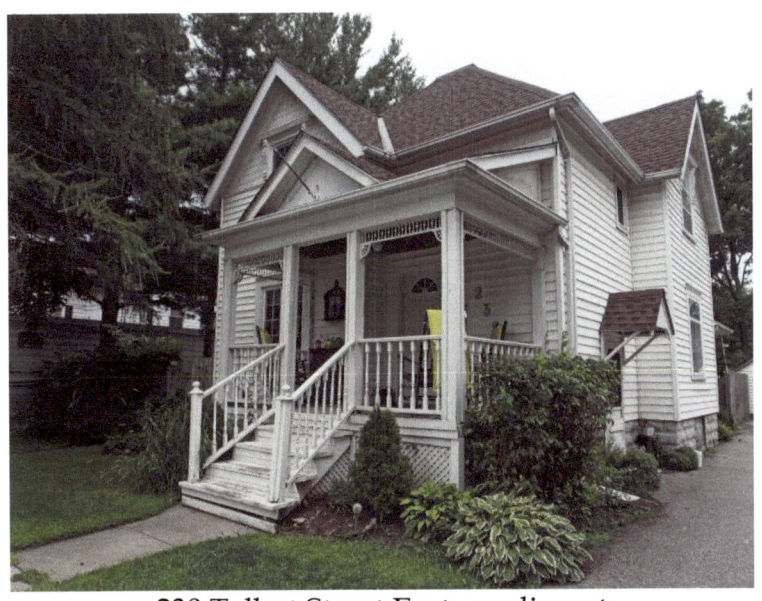

230 Talbot Street East - pediment

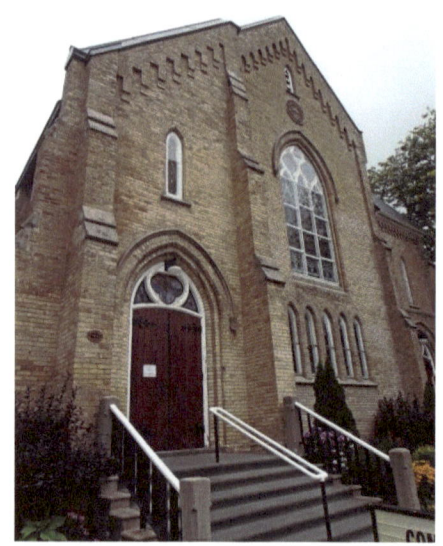

Talbot Street East – St. Paul's United Church
(Former Methodist Church of Canada 1874)

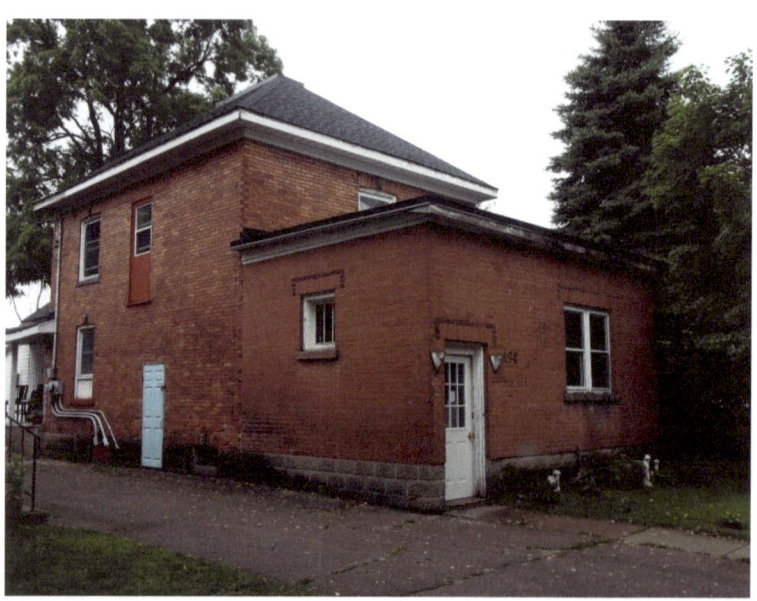

194 Talbot Street East – hipped roof on two-storey section

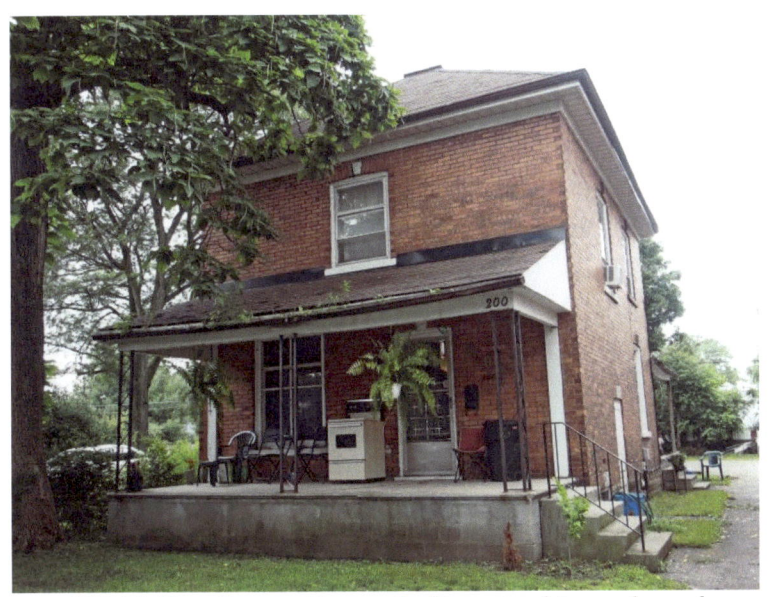

200 Talbot Street East – Italianate, hipped roof

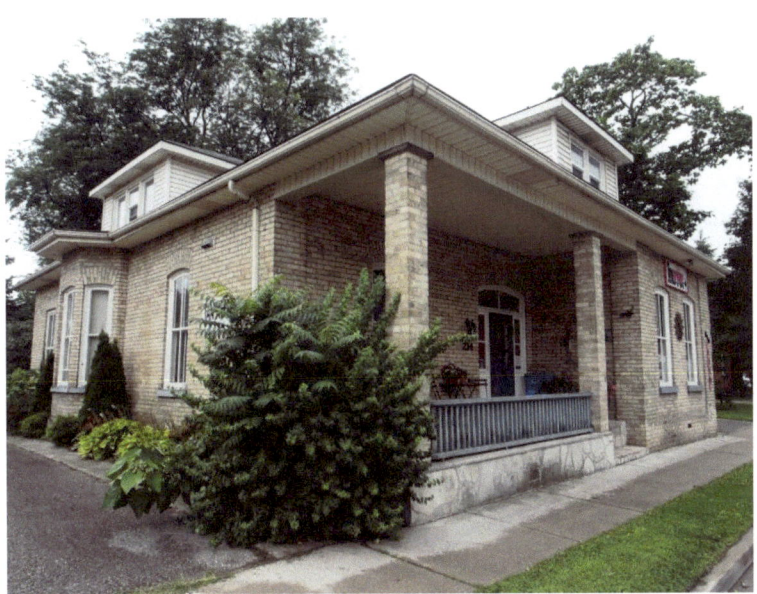

214 Talbot Street East – dormers in roof

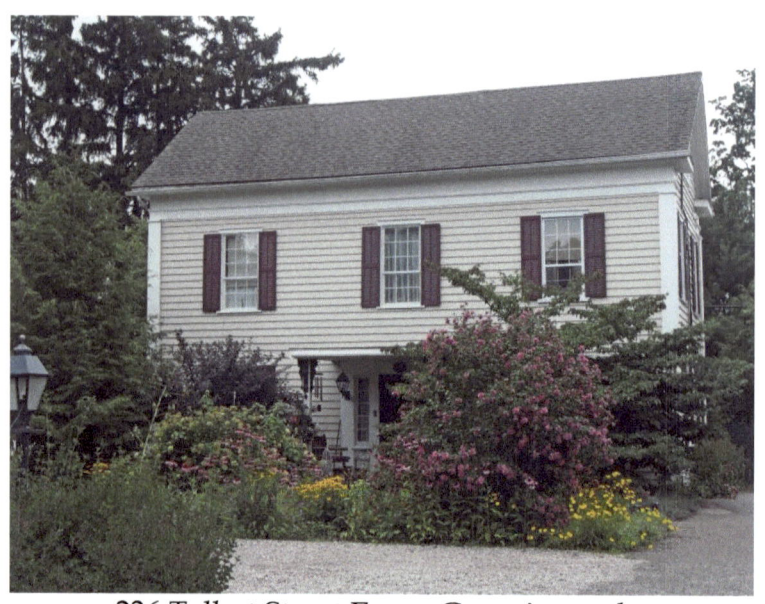

236 Talbot Street East – Georgian style,
Sweet Magnolia House Bed and Breakfast

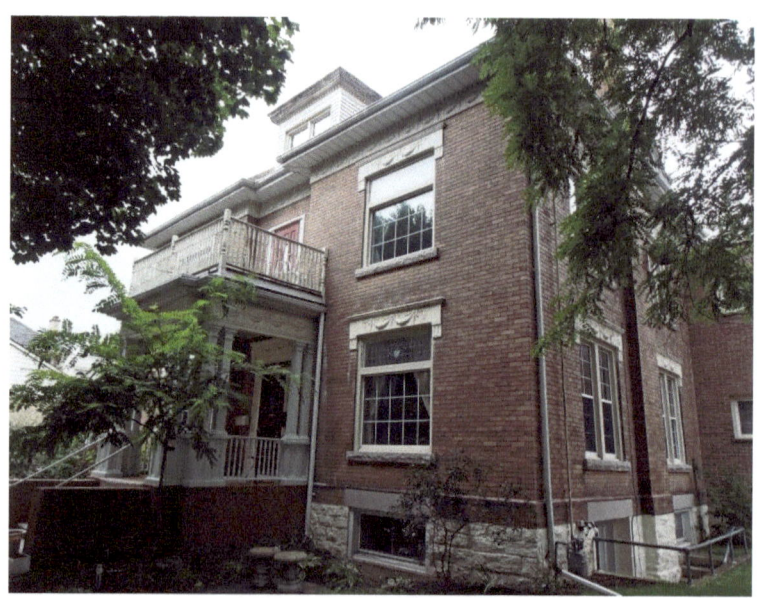

258 Talbot Street East
Brookside Manor Seniors Retirement Home

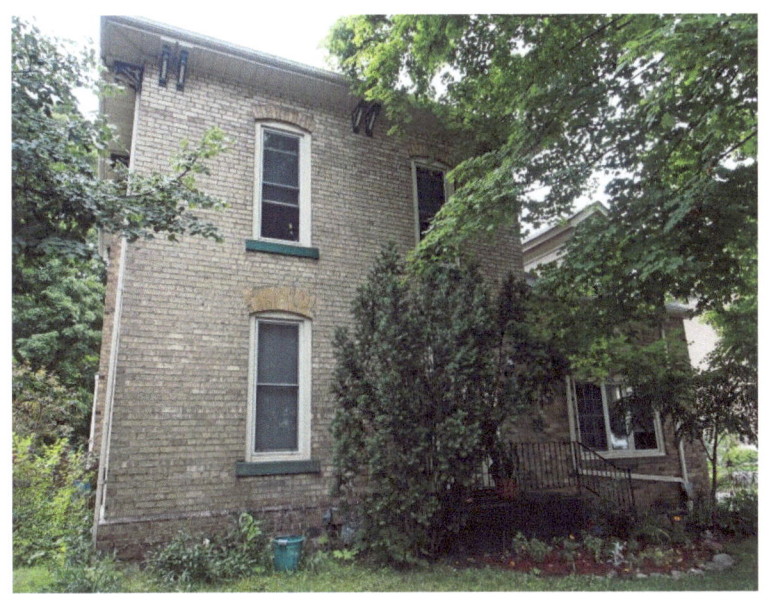

274 Talbot Street East – Italianate, paired cornice brackets

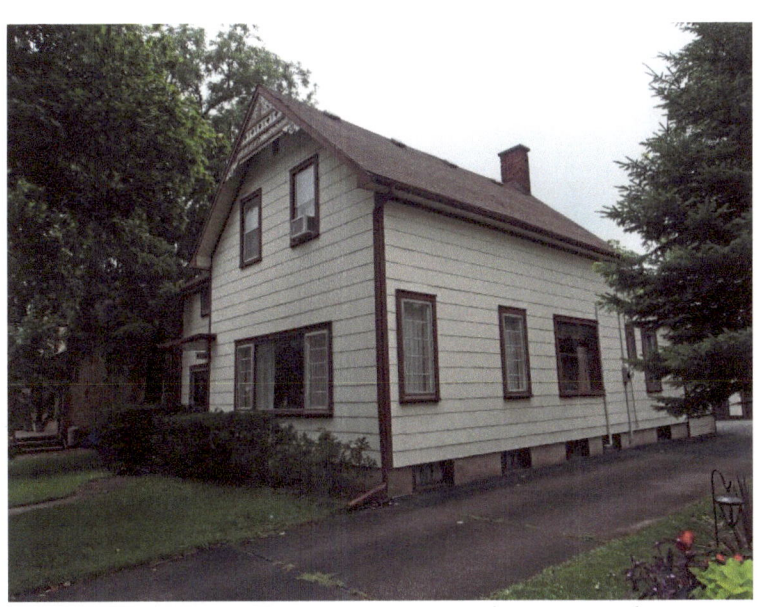

306 Talbot Street East – Gothic Revival,
vergeboard trim on gable

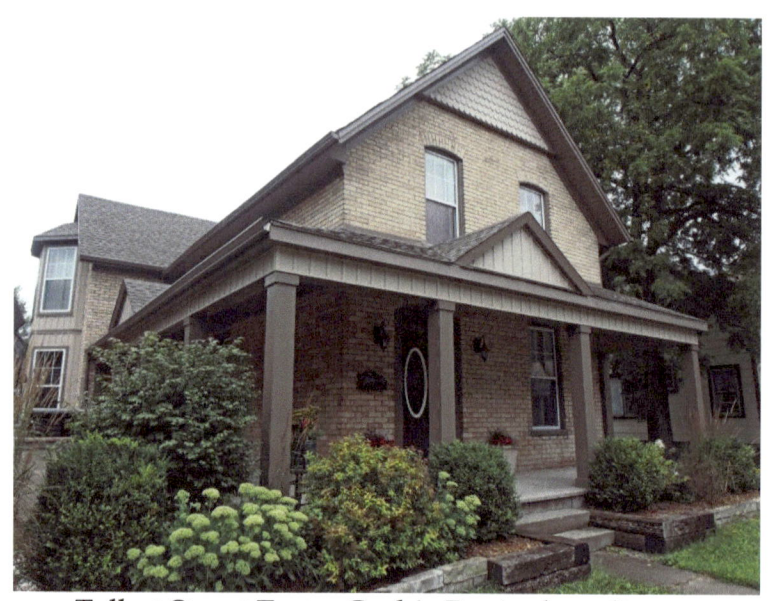

Talbot Street East – Gothic Revival, pediment

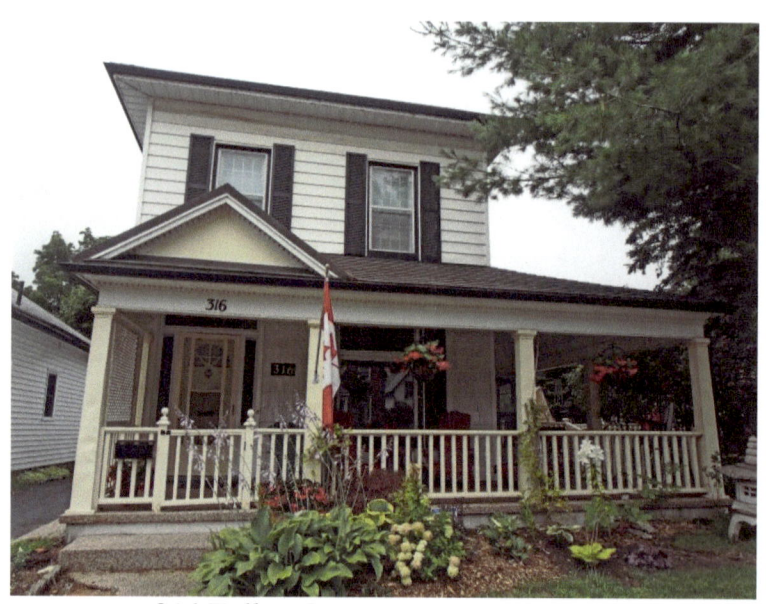

316 Talbot Street East – pediment

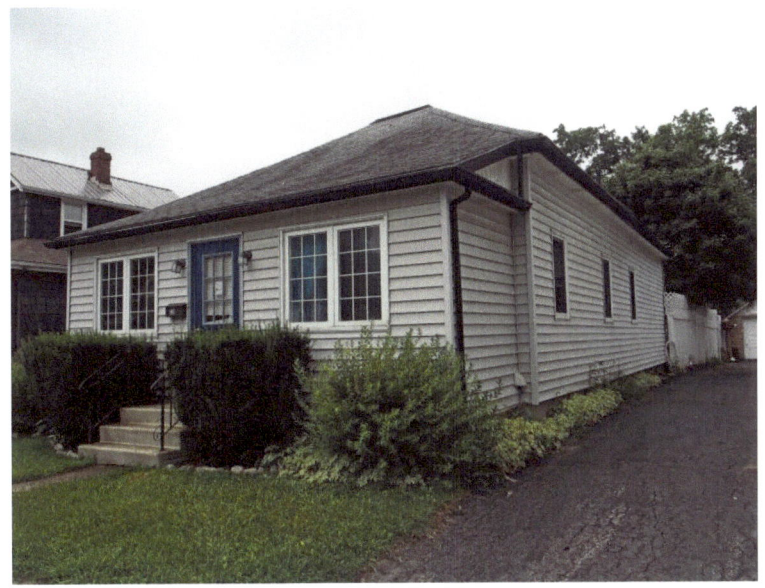

Talbot Street East – Regency Cottage

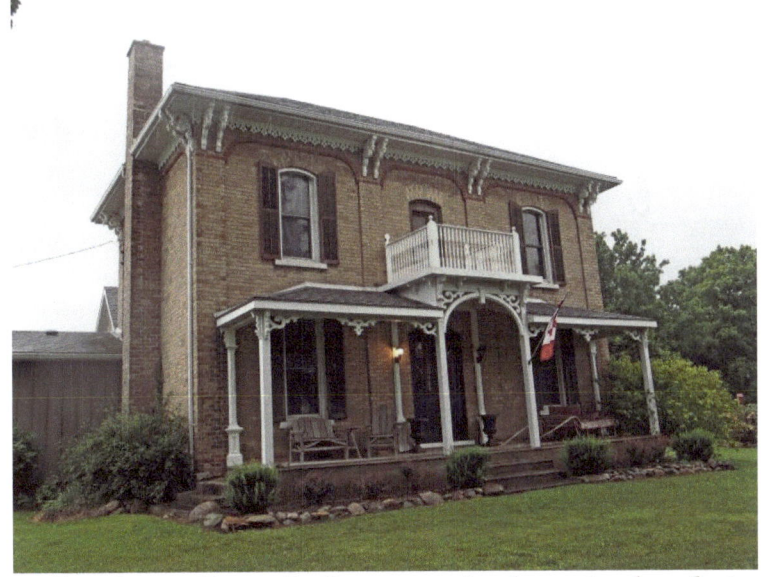

Talbot Street East – Italianate, paired cornice brackets,
balcony on second floor, decorative cornice trim

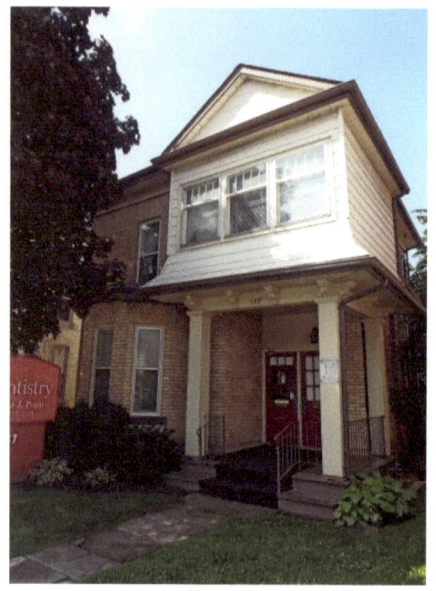

147 Talbot Street East

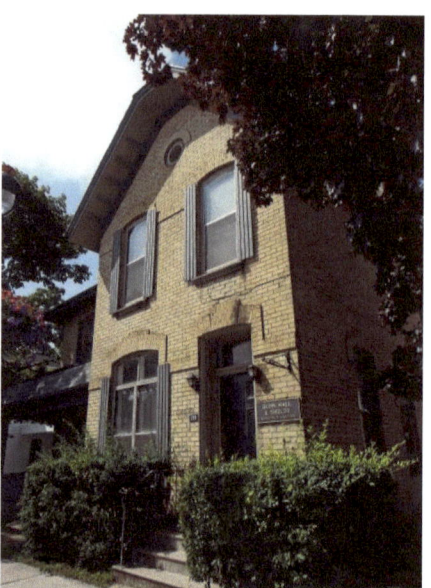

139 Talbot Street East

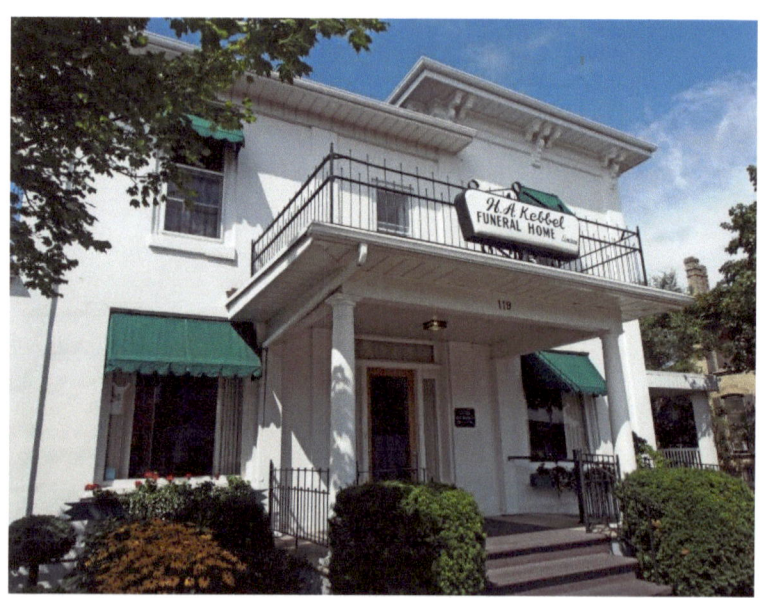

119 Talbot Street East – H. A. Kebbel Funeral Home

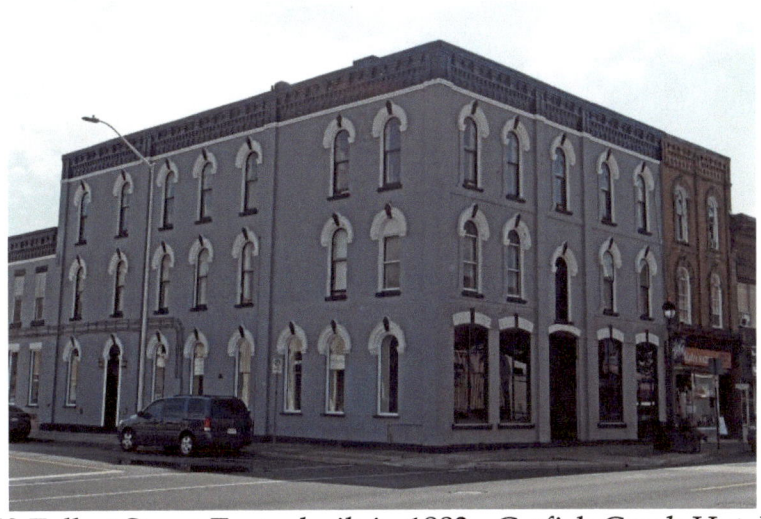

62 Talbot Street East – built in 1883 - Catfish Creek Hotel, former names Central Hotel and Kennedy Central Hotel – three storeys crowned by an ornate brick cornice

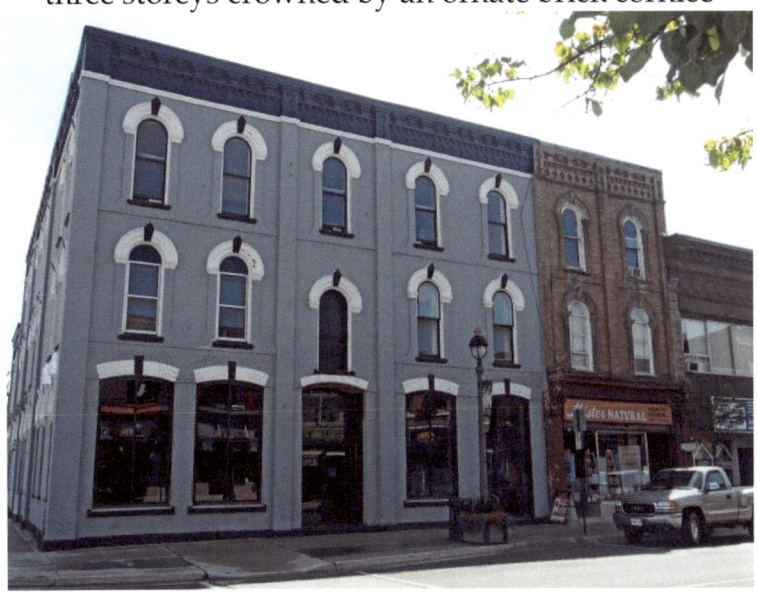

Romanesque style windows with stylishly carved stone architraves with keystones

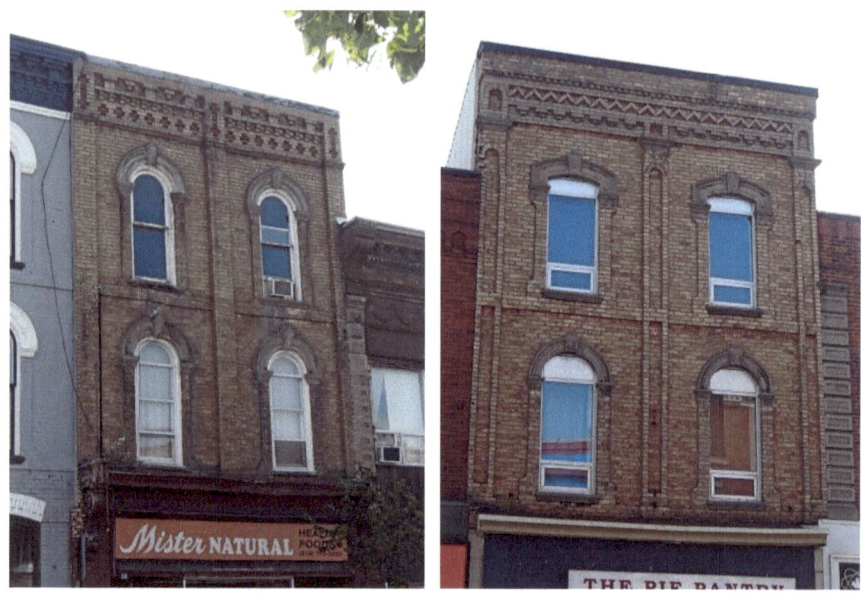

Dichromatic brickwork, pilasters

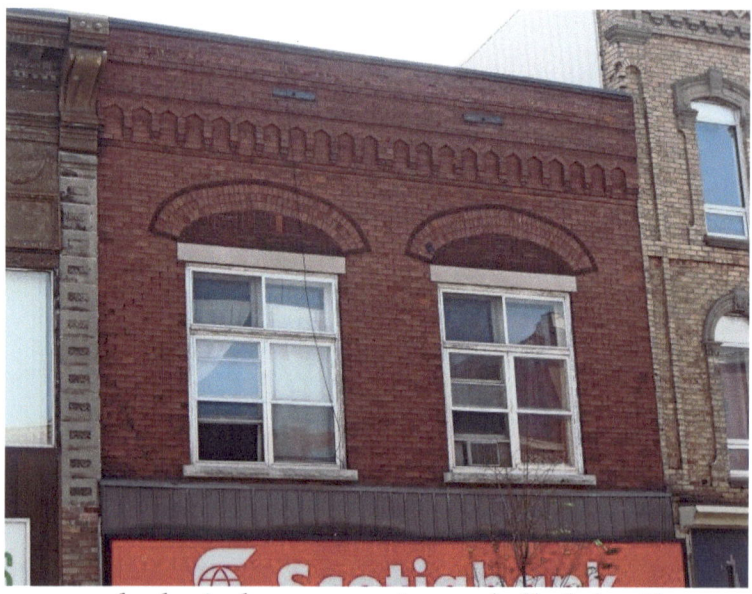

arched window voussoirs, corbelled dentils

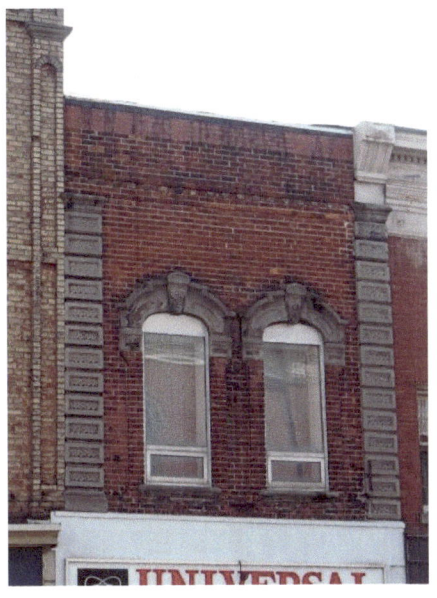

Decorative architraves and keystones

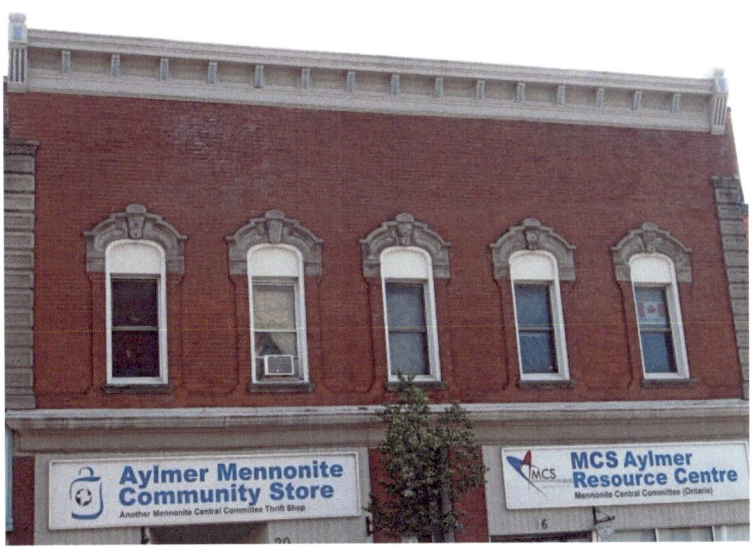

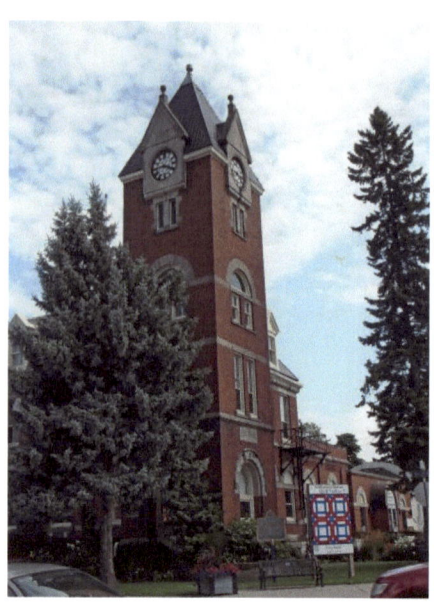

46 Talbot Street West - Aylmer Town Hall and Municipal
Offices – clock tower, dormers, cupola,
arched window voussoirs

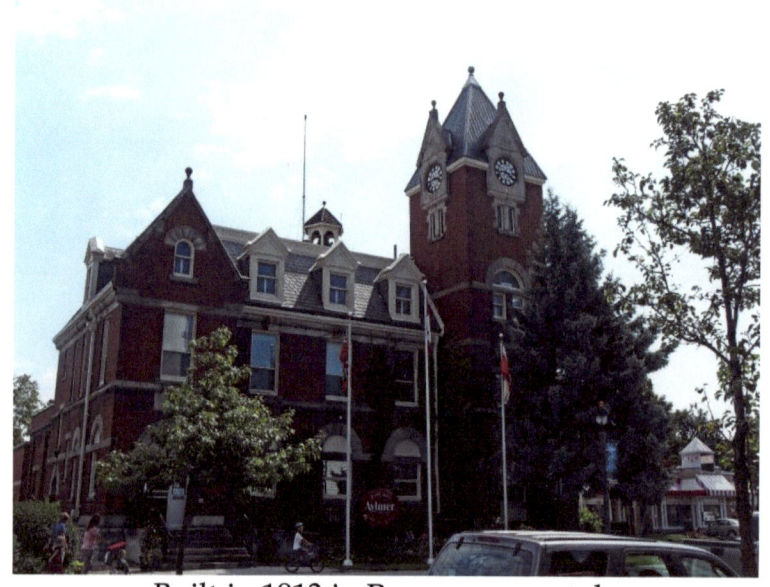

Built in 1913 in Romanesque style

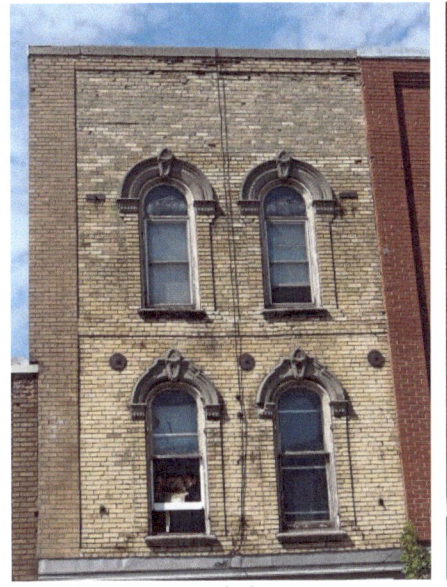

Architraves with keystones

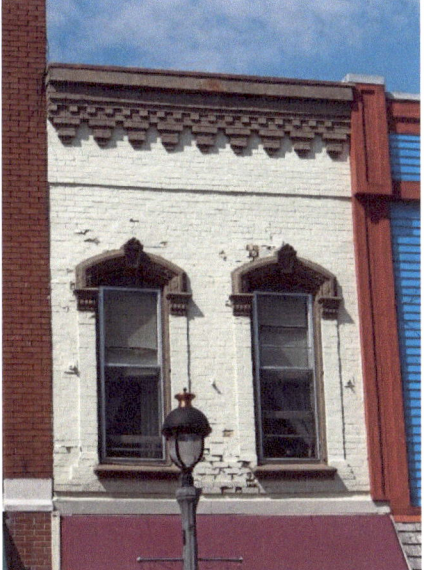

corbelled dentils

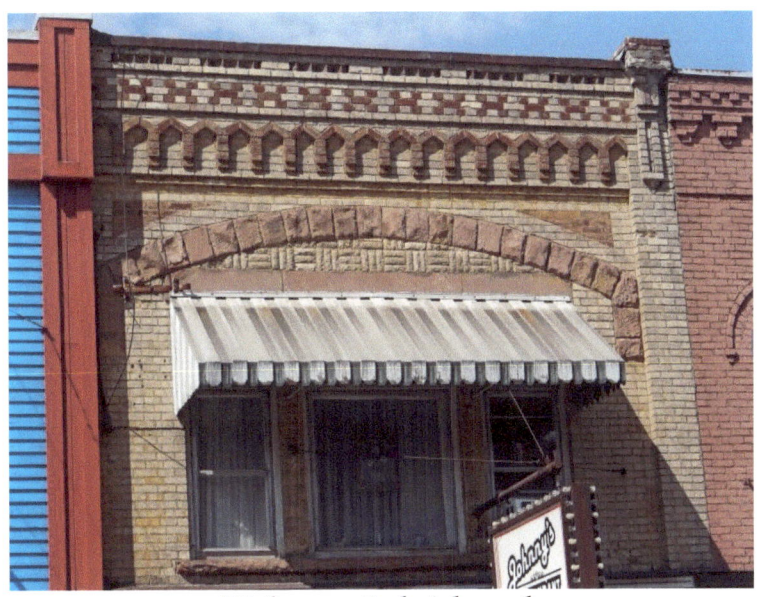

Dichromatic brickwork

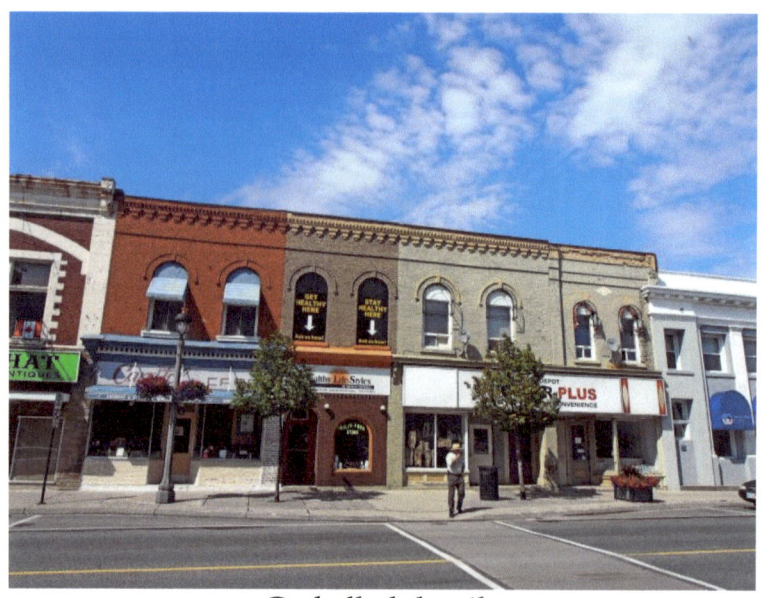

Corbelled dentils

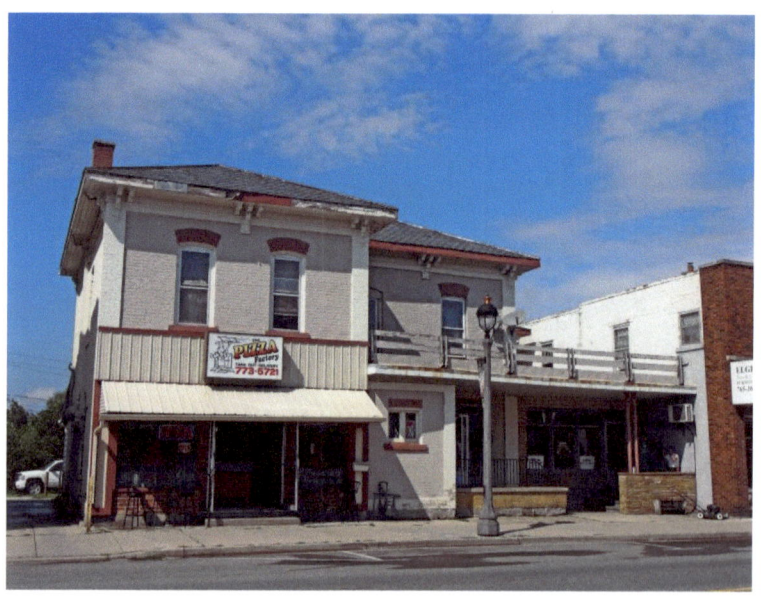

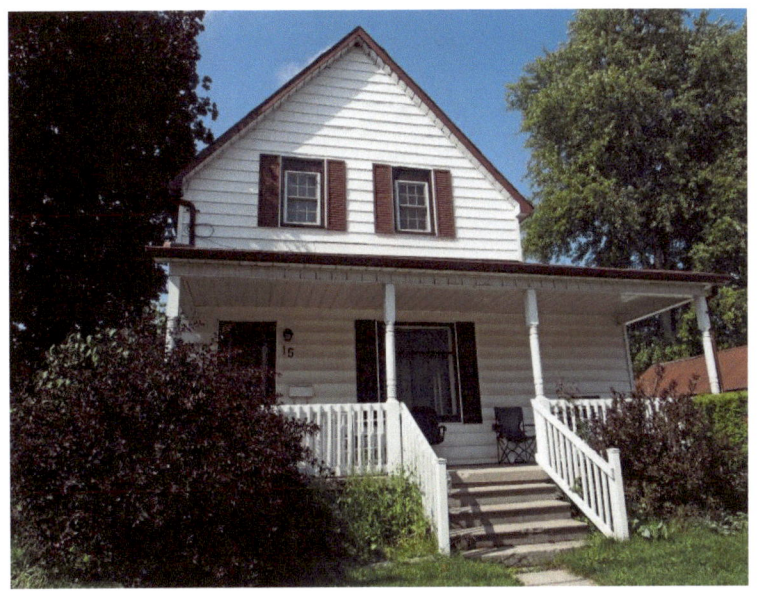

15 Spruce Street - Gothic

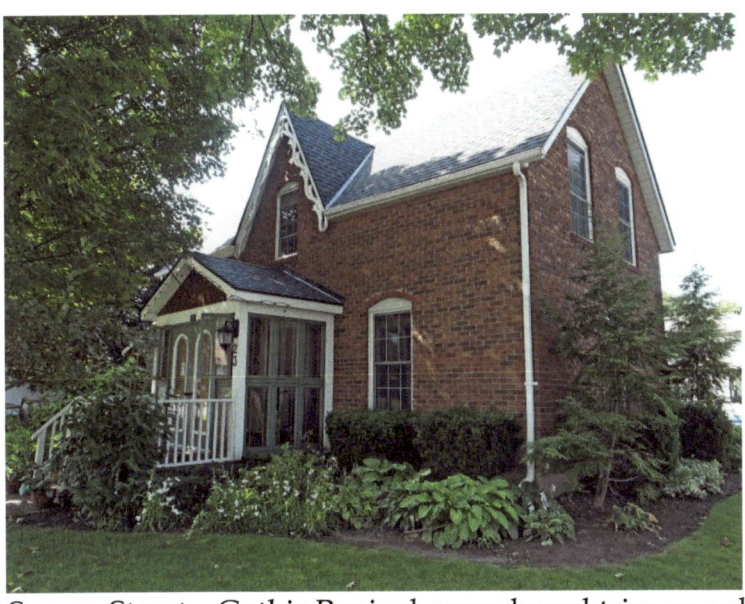

23 Spruce Street – Gothic Revival, vergeboard trim on gable

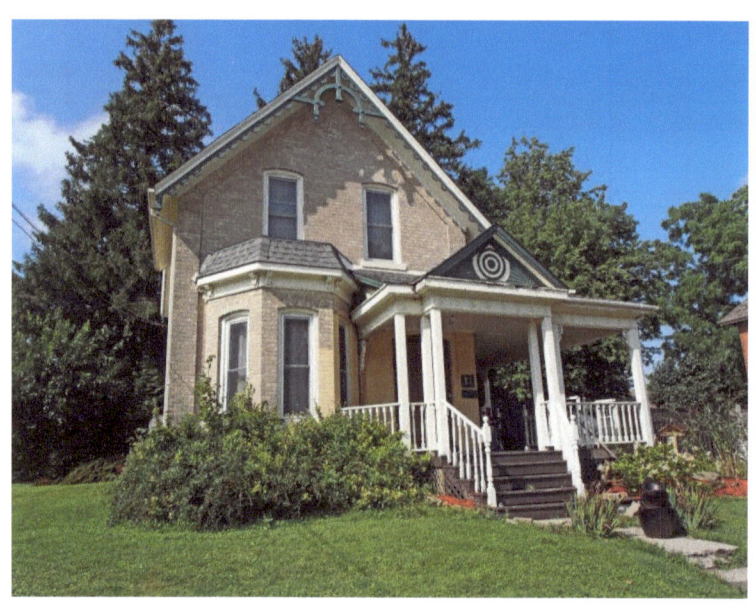

11 Walnut Street – Gothic Revival, vergeboard trim on gables, bay window, pediment with decorative tympanum

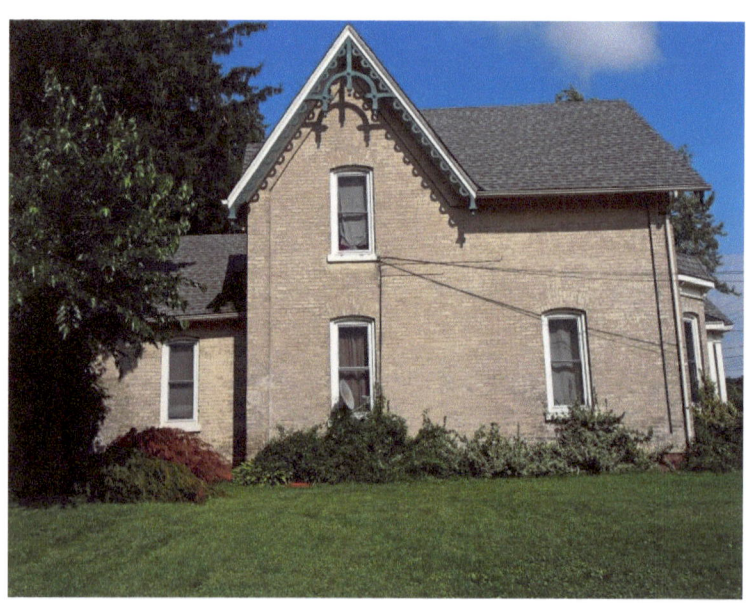

Architectural Terms

Architrave: The lowest division of the entablature (the entire horizontal mass above the columns) in classical architecture. The main lintel or beam spanning from column to column. Example: 62 Talbot Street East	
Brackets: a decorative or weight-bearing structural element which forms a right angle with one side against a wall and the other under a projecting surface such as an eave or roof. Example: Talbot Street East	
Buttress: a masonry structure built against or projecting from a wall which serves to support or reinforce the wall. In Canadian architecture, they are sometimes used for decoration. Example: Trinity Anglican Church	
Cornice: originally the wooden overhang of the roof. With the use of stone, brick, iron and steel, the cornice is any projecting shelf at the top of a ceiling or roof. They can be very decorative. Example: Talbot Street East	
Dentil Moulding: an even series of rectangles used as ornamental decoration in cornices. Example: Trinity Anglican Church	
Dichromatic brickwork: the use of two colours of brick, tile or slate to decorate a façade. Trichromatic is the use of three colours. Example: Downtown	
Dormer: (French for "sleep") a gable end window that pierces through the plane of a sloping roof surface to create usable space in the top floor or attic of a building by adding headroom. Example:	

Gable: the triangular portion of a wall between the edges of a sloping roof. Example: 116 Sydenham Street East	
Hipped Roof: a roof where all sides slope downwards to the walls with no gables. Example: 302 John Street North	
Iron Cresting: A decorative ornament along the top of a roof. Iron cresting was popular in the Baroque era and also in Italianate, Victorian, Second Empire and Queen Anne styles of architecture. Example: 20 Pine Street	
Keystones and Voussoirs: a voussoir is a wedge-shaped element used in building an arch. A keystone is the central stone that locks all the stones into position, allowing the arch to bear weight. A keystone is often enlarged and embellished. Example: downtown	
Lancet Window: a tall, narrow window with a pointed arch at its top. Example: Trinity Anglican Church	
Palladian Window: a large window that is divided into three sections with the centre section larger than the two side sections and usually arched. Example: 32 Pine Street	

Pediment: a triangular section above the horizontal structure (entablature), typically supported by columns. The inside of the triangle is called the tympanum. Example: 124 Sydenham Street East	
Pilaster: a slightly projecting column built into or applied to the face of a wall for additional structural support. Example: see Page 57	
Quoin: masonry blocks at the corner of a wall, often a decorative feature, usually larger or of a different colour than the rest of the wall. Example: 310 Sydenham Street East	
Turret: a small tower that projects from the wall of a building. Example: 111 Sydenham Street East	
Vergeboard and Finial: also called bargeboards – hang from the projecting end of a roof and are often elaborately carved and ornamented. **Finial:** ornament added to the top of a gable, pinnacle, canopy or spire – a Gothic element. Example: 40 Water Street	
Window Hood: A **hood** is the piece found above window openings, usually of an ornate design, and covers the top third of the opening. Hoods are commonly placed above arched or curved openings on both windows and doors. Example: 113 Sydenham Street East	

Building Styles

Edwardian, 1900-1930 – This style bridges the ornate and elaborate styles of the Victorian era and the simplified styles of the 20th century. Balanced facades, simple roof lines, dormer windows, large front porches, and smooth brick surfaces are its characteristics. Example: 32 Pine Street	
Georgian, before 1860 – This style began with the British King Georges in the 18th century. These buildings have balanced facades around a central door, medium-pitched gable roofs, and small paned windows. Example: 236 Talbot Street East	
Gothic Revival, 1830-1890 – These decorative buildings have sharply-pitched gables with highly detailed vergeboards, pointed-arch window openings, and dichromatic brickwork. It is a common style in Ontario. Example: 116 Sydenham Street East	
Italianate, 1850-1900 – It has wide-bracketed eaves, belvederes, wrap-around verandahs. Example: 186 Sydenham Street East	
Queen Anne, 1885-1900 – This style is distinguished by an irregular outline featuring a combination of an offset tower, broad gables, projecting two-storey bays, verandahs, multi-sloped roofs, and tall, decorative chimneys. A mixture of brick and wood is common. Windows often have one large single-paned bottom sash and small panes in the upper sash. Example: 111 Sydenham Street East	

Renaissance Revival (1870 - 1910) - The Renaissance Palazzo was a three or four storey building with a rusticated (very large masonry blocks with deep joints and decorated with rough or bold finishes) ground floor, and regularized understated windows on two upper levels, always finished by an elaborate cornice. The Renaissance saw the development of a graceful and balanced adaptation of the Greek styles. In Ontario, the Renaissance was revived in commercial buildings, banks, offices, and churches in many towns. Most of the Renaissance Revival buildings are designed without columns while those with columns and pilasters are more ornate. Example: 24 Pine Street	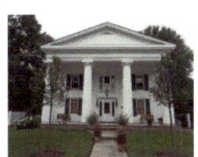
Romanesque Revival, 1880-1910 – This style hearkens back to medieval architecture of the 11th and 12th centuries with a heavy appearance, blocky towers and rounded arches. Example: Town Hall Municipal Offices, 46 Talbot Street West	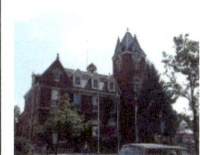

www.ingramcontent.com/pod-product-compliance
Lightning Source LLC
Chambersburg PA
CBHW040841180526
45159CB00001B/271